HAWAI'I'S BEST LOCAL
D I S H E S

Jean Watanabe Hee

MUTUAL PUBLISHING

All rights reserved
Library of Congress Catalog Card
Number: 2002108939

First Printing, October 2002
Second Printing, November 2002
Third Printing, April 2003
Fourth Printing, March 2004
4 5 6 7 8 9

ISBN 1-56647-570-8

Photography by Ray Wong
Art direction by Jane Hopkins with Sistenda Yim
Design by Sistenda Yim

Mutual Publishing
1215 Center Street, Suite 210
Honolulu, Hawai'i 96816
Ph: (808) 732-1709
Fax: (808) 734-4094
e-mail: mutual@mutualpublishing.com
www.mutualpublishing.com

Printed in Korea

Dedication

To my husband, Don, who always preferred eating at home
rather than at a restaurant.

Table of Contents

Recipes with * are Quick and Easy

SEAFOOD

Quick and Easy

Acknowledgments

I want to thank all my relatives, neighbors and friends who contributed their best and favorite recipes. It was difficult to select the best of any dish since each individual has his own preference, but I tried to get as many responses as I could for the final selection. I thank all the people who taste-tested and gave me their opinions.

Thank you to Audrey Mijo and Ruby Saito, my neighbors and good friends, who helped me by their willingness to become involved in the creation of this cookbook. Audrey's grandmother, Mrs. Mitoe, was a former caterer and Audrey, as a young girl, often assisted in the preparation. I appreciated her suggestions and input.

To the Chinese side of my family, thank you for contributing your best Chinese recipes. To the Japanese side of my family, thank you for the Japanese recipes. To all the younger nieces and nephews, thank you for the Mexican, Italian and "quick and easy" recipes that you like.

I want to especially thank my husband, Don, who is my greatest supporter and who had to live through all the hundreds of testing of recipes.

Finally, I want to thank my publisher, Bennett Hymer, for his support and encouragement. Thank you to all the helpful and friendly staff at Mutual Publishing.

Introduction

The idea of creating a cookbook for Hawai'i's best main dishes had been suggested by many people. At book signings for my cookbook, *Hawai'i's Best Local Desserts,* young couples mentioned that they'd like a cookbook on local-type dinner recipes. My friends and relatives also wanted one for their kitchen so they could get rid of their little scraps of paper with hastily written directions or trying to remember which cookbook had that best recipe for a particular dish.

Testing and selecting the best local recipes was a formidable task! There are so many wonderful mouth-watering dishes here, encompassing all ethnic groups. The food is great in Hawai'i! And so many ways to prepare them! For example, I consulted my sister-in-law, Rose, and other Filipino friends on how they prepare their pork adobo. I found so many variations. After testing many, I selected the one Steve Araki shared with me which he had gotten from a good friend and cook.

Included in this cookbook are quick and easy recipes that can be whipped up in less than 30 minutes after a busy day at work. All recipes in this book were tested. Some recipes can be prepped the night before and easily cooked the next day. There are recipes that are more time-consuming but are so delicious. There are pot-luck recipes for taking to the beach or homes of friends and relatives. I also included some unusual recipes, such as "Black Bean Salmon Head," which tastes better than it sounds. Have you ever seen salmon fish heads in the supermarket and wondered what to do with them?

The size of the cookbook made it very difficult to select which recipes would be included. Everyone's taste is different and our main dishes here can be in many forms. A bowl of hearty Portuguese bean soup is a main meal by itself or, as in the Asian style, we may have several entrées for our family meal. I tried to include a variety of dishes that are enjoyed by the locals who live here.

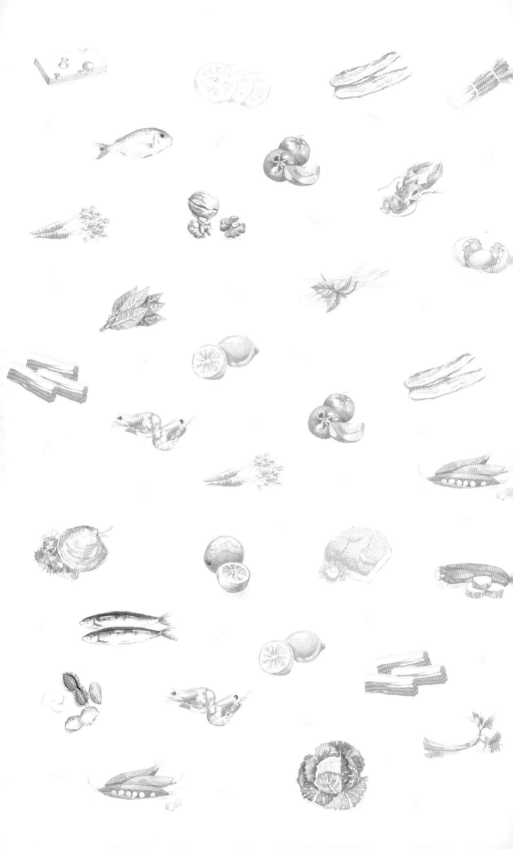

· BEEF ·

Beef Tips

- Store meat immediately in the coldest part of your refrigerator, or freeze as soon as possible.
- Use ground meat promptly, since it deteriorates more quickly than other types of meat.
- Select meat packages that are wrapped with no tears or punctures.
- Do not buy any meat that has turned gray in color or has an off odor.
- Look for the sell-by date on the label and purchase meat before or on the date listed.
- Marbling in meats refers to the small flecks of fat throughout the lean. More marbling means higher quality in flavor and juiciness. It also indicates higher fat and calories.
- Be careful not to overcook meats. Leaner meats, especially, with less marbling, can toughen easily.
- Supermarkets may call meat cuts by different names. If in doubt, ask for help from the meat personnel working there.
- The number of servings per pound will depend on the type of meat when it's cooked and the amount of bone and fat. The average is about 3 to 4 servings per pound. For very bony cuts of meat (i.e. spareribs, short ribs), allow about 1 to 1-1/2 servings per pound.
- Thaw meat slowly in the refrigerator, or quickly in the microwave, and not on the countertop at room temperature.
- Partially frozen raw meat is easier to cut into thin strips and slices.
- Wash all surfaces and utensils that come in contact with raw meat with hot, soapy water.

Shredded Barbecue Beef

yield: 4 servings

1 pound stew meat
1 onion, sliced
2 quarts water
1/2 cup catsup
2 teaspoons prepared mustard
1/4 cup brown sugar, packed
2 Tablespoons vinegar
2 Tablespoons French dressing
salt and pepper to taste

Cook stew meat and onions in water for 2 hours, or until tender. Remove meat. Leave 1 to 1-1/2 cups of liquid; drain the remainder. Shred meat and return to pot with liquid.

In another pot, mix catsup, mustard and the rest of the ingredients and simmer on low heat, covered, for 15 to 20 minutes. Add mixture to meat. Simmer, uncovered, to allow liquid to evaporate to desired consistency. Serve over steamed rice or on hamburger buns.

Beef Broccoli

yield: 4 servings

1 pound meat, sliced
2 teaspoons sugar
2 Tablespoons shoyu
1 Tablespoon ginger, crushed
2 Tablespoons sherry or whiskey
2 Tablespoons flour
2 pounds broccoli, sliced
1/2 teaspoon salt
1/2 cup water
oil for frying

Marinate meat with sugar, shoyu, ginger, sherry and flour. Set aside. Heat 1 teaspoon oil and stir-fry broccoli. Add salt and water. Simmer, covered, until tender and take out. (Do not overcook broccoli.) In the same pan, heat 1 Tablespoon oil and stir-fry meat for 2 minutes. Add broccoli and mix together until heated through.

Chopped Steak

yield: 4 to 6 servings

1 pound boneless sirloin steak, thinly sliced
oil for frying
1 clove garlic, crushed
1 onion, sliced
1 stalk celery, slivered
1 carrot, slivered
1 green pepper, slivered
1 tomato, cut in wedges
2 Tablespoons shoyu
1/2 teaspoon sugar
1/4 teaspoon salt
1/4 teaspoon pepper

Heat 1 Tablespoon oil in skillet. Lightly stir-fry vegetables (except tomato) for about 1 minute. Remove and set aside. Add 1 Tablespoon oil in the same pan and sauté garlic and stir-fry meat until almost done. Add shoyu, seasonings, vegetables and tomato. Cook until heated.

Beef Tomato

yield: 4 to 6 servings

1 pound beef (sirloin, flank, sirloin tip, round, etc.),
   thinly sliced
1 onion, wedged
2 stalks celery, cut diagonally in thick slices
2 green peppers, wedged
pinch of salt
1 to 2 tomatoes, wedged
2 stalks green onion, cut in 1-1/2-inch lengths
oil for frying

Marinade:
   1-inch piece fresh ginger, crushed
   1 clove garlic, crushed
   1/2 teaspoon sugar
   1/2 teaspoon salt
   2 Tablespoons shoyu
   1 Tablespoon sherry
   pinch of pepper
   1 Tablespoon cornstarch
   1 Tablespoon oil

Gravy:
   1 Tablespoon cornstarch
   1-1/2 teaspoons sugar
   1 teaspoon shoyu
   1/2 teaspoon Worcestershire™ sauce
   1 Tablespoon catsup (or more to your taste)

Soak beef slices in marinade for 15 to 20 minutes. Heat 2 teaspoons oil in pan or wok and stir-fry round onion, celery and bell pepper on medium-high heat for about 2 minutes. Season with salt to your taste. Add tomatoes and cook on additional minute. Remove from pan. Heat 2 teaspoons oil in the same pan and saute beef until medium rare. Remove garlic and ginger. Add the stir-fried vegetables, green onion and gravy. Bring to a quick boil; turn heat off.

Butter Yaki

yield: 4 servings

1 pound tender meat, thinly sliced
1 pound chicken breasts, boneless and skinless, thinly
sliced
1 package bean sprouts (10-oz.)
1 onion, thinly sliced
1 zucchini, cut into 2-1/2-inch lengths, then cut into "sticks"
1 tray mushrooms (8-oz.), sliced
1/2 block butter
Sauce:
1/4 cup shoyu
1/4 cup mirin
1/4 cup sugar
1/4 cup daikon, peeled and grated
1/4 cup apple, peeled and grated
2 limes, cut in halves (optional)

Prepare sauce first. Cook all sauce ingredients, except for limes, for a few minutes. Cool and set aside in 4 individual serving dishes. (Individuals may squeeze in own lime juice, if preferred, before dipping cooked meat and vegetables into the sauce.)

Use an electric skillet set at 250°F at dinner table. (Temperature may be adjusted while you cook.) Add some butter to skillet and place some bean sprouts and onion slices to begin cooking. When bean sprouts and onions are about half done, add mushrooms and zucchini slices, adding more butter as needed. Cook thinly sliced meat and chicken last. Eat while it is hot, dipping in individual dishes of prepared sauce. Add more vegetables and meat in skillet.

Variation: Add other types of vegetables, such as Chinese cabbage, green onion, watercress, cut in 2-inch lengths.

Note: This is a family favorite! The sauce is yummy and everything is freshly cooked and hot.

Meat Juhn

yield: 2 to 3 servings

1 pound meat (i.e. sirloin tip, flank steak, etc.), thinly
sliced
3 eggs, beaten
1/2 cup flour
2 Tablespoons oil for frying

Marinade:
4 Tablespoons shoyu
1 Tablespoon minced green onion
1/2 teaspoon sugar
1/2 teaspoon toasted sesame seeds
1/2 teaspoon minced garlic,
1/2 teaspoon sesame seed oil
pinch of pepper

Combine marinade ingredients and soak beef in sauce for 1 hour. Dredge meat
in flour, dip in eggs and fry in hot oil until brown on both sides. (Add more
oil as needed.) Drain on paper towel. Slice and serve.

Note: Serve with Ko Choo Jung Dipping Sauce, if desired.

Ko Choo Jung Dipping Sauce:
1/3 cup shoyu
1/3 cup vinegar
1/3 cup sugar
3 Tablespoons ko choo jung
2 Tablespoons toasted sesame seeds
Hawaiian chili pepper, cut in half (optional)

Combine all ingredients.

Jumbo's Restaurant's Beef Stew

yield: 6 to 8 servings

3 to 4 pounds stew meat, cut into 1-1/2-inch cubes
salt and pepper to season
4 cloves garlic, crushed
1 Tablespoon oil
1/2 cup red wine
1 large onion, cut in chunks
5 stalks celery, cut in 1/2-inch slices
2 Tablespoons sugar
2 Tablespoons salt
1 teaspoon black pepper
2 bay leaves
1 can Hunt's™ tomato paste (6-oz.)
4 carrots, cut into large pieces
3 to 4 potatoes, cut into large pieces
4 Tablespoons cornstarch mixed with 4 Tablespoons water

Heat oil and braise stew meat on medium-high heat for approximately 5 minutes, or until brown. (Lightly salt and pepper meat while cooking.) Add garlic and sauté a few minutes to release the flavor. Add wine and sauté for another 3 to 5 minutes, or until alcohol is evaporated. Add onions and celery and cook for a few minutes.

Cover the meat with water (about 14 to 16 cups water). Add spices, bay leaves and tomato paste; bring to boil. Lower heat to medium-low, cover, and cook for approximately 1 hour, or until meat is tender. Add carrots and cook for approximately 10 minutes. Add potatoes, continue cooking until vegetables are tender. Thicken with cornstarch mixture and simmer for a few minutes.

Note: This is a reduced version of Jumbo's Restaurant's award-winning famous beef stew. Jumbo's made this and their fried min the favorites of local folks. Jumbo's is just a memory now, but their beef stew is still great!

Hamburger Steak With Gravy, "Loco Moco" Style

yield: 4 servings

1 pound lean ground beef
1 slice bread, cubed
2 Tablespoons milk or water
1 egg, slightly beaten
1/2 cup chopped onion
1 Tablespoon tomato catsup
1 teaspoon salt
dash of pepper

Gravy:
1 cup beef or chicken broth
3 Tablespoons flour mixed with 4 Tablespoons water
salt and pepper to taste

Hot cooked rice
4 eggs, fried "over easy"

Mix bread cubes with milk or water until bread is softened. Mix together ground beef, softened bread cubes and rest of ingredients. Mix well; form into patties. Pan fry or broil to desired doneness.

Place cooked hamburgers on a warm platter and keep warm while preparing the gravy. Remove oil, leaving brown particles in pan. Pour broth into pan and heat to boiling, stirring and loosening brown particles. Mix flour with water to make a smooth paste. Slowly add to heated broth, stirring constantly, until smooth. Add salt and pepper.

Serve the hamburger steak on hot steamed rice, with a fried egg on the hamburger and gravy over all.

Lazy Day Steak

yield: 2 to 3 servings

2 pounds chuck steak
1 envelope onion soup mix
1 can beer

Cut chuck steak into portion size pieces. Combine all ingredients in baking dish. Cover and bake 3 hours at 300°F or until meat is tender and there is a rich gravy.

Variation: Add potatoes and carrots in the last hour of cooking.

Osso Buco

yield: 6 servings

6 veal shanks
1/3 cup flour
1 teaspoon salt
1/4 teaspoon pepper
2 Tablespoons olive oil
1 cup finely chopped onion
1 cup carrots, cut in rounds, 1/4-inch thickness
1 cup finely chopped celery
2 cloves garlic, minced
1 can tomatoes (28-oz.), coarsely chopped
1 cup white wine
1 teaspoon dried basil leaves
1 teaspoon dried thyme leaves
1 bay leaf
3 Tablespoons chopped parsley

Wipe veal shanks with a damp paper towel; set aside. Combine flour, salt and pepper; coat veal and shake off excess flour. Heat olive oil in heavy pot. Sauté veal until nicely browned on all sides. Remove from pot and keep warm.

Add onions, carrots, celery and garlic to the pot. Sauté for about 5 minutes. Add tomatoes, wine, basil, thyme and bay leaf. Mix well and bring to a boil. Return veal to pot and simmer, covered, for about 2 hours. Add parsley, transfer to a serving dish.

Variation: Substitute veal shanks with beef shanks.

Note: This is one of the best recipes that I have tasted for this dish!

Shish Kabob

yield: 4 to 6 servings

2 pounds sirloin steak or chicken breasts, cubed
1 large bell pepper, cubed
1 large onion, cubed
2 tomatoes cut in bite-size pieces, or cherry tomatoes, halved
1 can whole mushrooms (4-oz.)
20 skewers, approximately, soaked in water

Marinade:
1/4 cup shoyu
1/4 cup oil
2 teaspoons salt
1/2 teaspoon pepper
1 clove garlic, crushed
juice of 1 lemon

Soak meat and onions in marinade for about 2 hours. Place meat alternately with vegetables on skewers and top end with mushrooms. Cook over a hibachi.

Sukiyaki

yield: 4 servings

1 pound beef or boned chicken breast, thinly sliced
1 Tablespoon oil
1/3 cup sugar
1/2 cup shoyu
1/4 cup beer or sherry
1 onion, thinly sliced
1/2 cup chicken broth
1 can Sukiyaki No Tomo (8-3/4-oz.), slice contents if needed
1/2 block firm tofu, cubed (half of 20-oz. container)
1 bunch long rice, softened in water and cut in 2-inch
  lengths (2-oz.)
2 cups watercress, cut in 1-1/2-inch pieces
1 to 2 stalks green onions, cut in 1-1/2-inch pieces

Heat oil in skillet. Brown beef or chicken. Add sugar, shoyu and beer; simmer for a few minutes. Add onion and cook until tender. Add all other ingredients (except green vegetables). Cook 2 to 3 minutes. (Add more chicken broth if necessary.) Add green vegetables; cook until watercress is soft and tender.

Wiki Wiki Chili

yield: 4 servings

8 slices Portuguese sausage

1 pound ground beef

1 can tomato sauce (8-oz.)

1 cup catsup

1 cup water

1 to 2 teaspoons chili powder

1 teaspoon shoyu

1 can kidney beans, slightly drained (15-1/2-oz.)

1 teaspoon cornstarch mixed with 2 teaspoons water

Slice Portuguese sausage in small pieces and fry. Add hamburger and cook until brown. Drain excess oil. Add tomato sauce, catsup, water, chili powder and shoyu. Bring to a boil and cook on medium-low heat for 15 minutes. Add kidney beans and bring to a boil. Slowly add cornstarch mixture to chili, stirring to thicken more or less according to your taste.

Quick Corned Beef and Cabbage

yield: 4 servings

1 can corned beef (12-oz.)
1 onion, sliced
1 Tablespoon oil
1 small head cabbage, cut in chunks
salt and pepper to season

Heat oil and sauté onion. Add corned beef and cook for about a minute. Add cabbage. (Add a little water for moisture if necessary.) Cover and cook until cabbage is softened. Season with salt and pepper (or with sugar and shoyu, if preferred).

Tofu With Ground Beef and Miso

yield: 2 to 3 servings

1 container firm tofu (20-oz.), drained, cut in half and sliced
   into 6 pieces
cornstarch for dredging
2 Tablespoons oil
1/2 pound ground beef (ground turkey or pork)
1 stalk green onion, chopped
3 Tablespoons miso
1-1/2 Tablespoons sugar
1 Tablespoon shoyu
1 Tablespoon or 1 envelope dashi-no-moto
1 cup water

Coat tofu with cornstarch and fry. Set aside on paper towel to drain.

Fry beef and onions. Make paste of miso, sugar and shoyu. Add to hamburger.
Add 1 envelope dashi-no-moto and 1 cup water. Simmer for 10 to 15 minutes.
Lay tofu on plate. Pour sauce over tofu.

Note: Ruby Saito contributed this very delicious combination of beef, tofu and miso.

Baked Spaghetti

yield: 12 to 15 servings

2 pounds hamburger
2 teaspoons oil
1 onion, diced
1 clove garlic, diced
1 green pepper, diced
salt to season
2 cans (8-oz.) tomato sauce
1 can tomato soup (10-3/4-oz.)
1 can water (use tomato soup can)
1 large envelope spaghetti sauce mix (3-oz.)
1/2 pound cheddar cheese, grated
1 package spaghetti (16-oz.), cooked according to package
directions

Heat oil in frying pan; fry hamburger, onion, garlic and green pepper until browned and cooked. Salt to taste. Add tomato sauce, tomato soup, water and spaghetti sauce mix and simmer for about 30 minutes.

Place cooked spaghetti in a 10x14-inch roasting pan. Pour cooked mixture over spaghetti. Sprinkle cheese on top and bake at 350°F until cheese is browned and melted, about 20 to 30 minutes.

Note: This is great for potluck! I made this many times when the kids were little and all the cousins got together for a swim in the pool.

Kalbi

yield: 4 to 6 servings

4 pounds short ribs, thick cut

Marinade:
1/2 cup shoyu
1/4 cup sugar
1 Tablespoon ko choo jung sauce bean paste
4 cloves garlic, diced
1 Tablespoon julienne cut ginger
1 teaspoon sesame oil
4 Tablespoons finely sliced green onion
1 teaspoon roasted sesame seeds

Slice and "butterfly" meaty part of rib. Score deeply but avoid cutting the bone. Place flat in a container. Mix marinade ingredients and marinate ribs for 1 to 2 hours. Turn every 15 minutes or use a well-sealed container which can be "flip-flopped." Either broil or grill, turning several times until done.

Note: Always a local favorite at tailgates or BBQ gatherings. This original recipe was shared by Carolyn Sur and has been a long-time favorite with her husband Ken's Korean side of the family.

Beef Tongue

yield: 4 to 6 servings

1 Beef tongue (3 to 4 pounds)
1 to 2 Tablespoons oil
3 cloves garlic, crushed
1 cup shoyu
3 cups water
1 Tablespoon cornstarch mixed with 1 Tablespoon water

Cover beef tongue with water and parboil for 1 hour. Rinse in cold water. Scrape off white outer skin.

In a large pot, heat oil and brown garlic. Add tongue and brown on all sides. Add shoyu and brown on all sides. Add shoyu and water until it covers the tongue. (The shoyu sauce is a mixture of 1 part shoyu and 3 parts water. If necessary, use ratio to add more sauce to cover the tongue.)

Boil for 2-1/2 to 3 hours or until soft. (Poke with chopstick to test softness.) Slice tongue in 1/2-inch thick slices. Remove 1 cup of the shoyu sauce from the pot and thicken with cornstarch mixture. Heat until thickened and pour over tongue slices.

Note: This dish was once considered a Chinese delicacy and was eaten mostly in restaurants because not many knew how to prepare it. I am pleased to say that I finally tasted the most delicious beef tongue recipe which was shared by Audrey Au. This is her family recipe that is a definite favorite among her six children and their families.

Crescent Roll Tacos

yield: 4 to 6 servings

1 pound ground beef
1 envelope taco sauce mix (1.25-oz.)
1 can tomato sauce (8-oz.)
1/3 cup water
2 tubes crescent rolls (8-oz. each)
1 package grated cheddar cheese (8-oz.)
olives and mushrooms, sliced (optional)

Brown hamburger and drain oil. Add taco seasoning, tomato sauce and 1/3 cup water. Simmer for 5 minutes.

Grease a 9x13-inch pan with oil. Roll out half of the crescent roll at a time into the pan. Line the pan. Pour hamburger mix over crescent rolls in pan. Put cheese, olives and mushroom over. Open the second can of rolls and place over hamburger mix. Bake at 425°F for about 15 minutes.

Note: Gladys Fuchigami introduced this popular potluck dish at one of our "get-togethers" and we all asked for the recipe. She recommends using a taco mix that advertises less sodium. It will be less salty.

Corned Beef With Cabbage

yield: 2-3 servings

2 pounds corned beef brisket
1 to 2 potatoes, cut in fourths
2 carrots, cut in thirds
1 onion, cut in fourths
1/2 head small cabbage, cut lengthwise in thirds

Place corned beef brisket in a large pot and cover with water. (If spice packet is provided, add to pot, if desired for added taste.) Bring water to boil. Skim off "scum." Reduce heat, cover pot and simmer for 2-1/2 to 3 hours, or until "fork tender." Add vegetables to the corned beef during the last 30 to 40 minutes. Slice corned beef and serve with vegetables.

Suggestion: Serve with prepared mustard or hot mustard.

Note: Do not overcook corned beef. It should be tender but firm enough to slice. This is often requested by Eric Watanabe for Grandma Watanabe to prepare for dinner. Very simple and a great main course.

Evie's Red Stew

yield: 6 to 8 servings

4 pounds beef short ribs, cut into pieces
flour for coating
oil for browning
1 can V8™ juice (48-oz.)
1 can beef broth (14-oz.)
1 teaspoon Tabasco™ sauce
1-1/2 pounds carrots, cut in chunks
2 pounds potatoes, cut in chunks
1 large onion, cut into 1-1/2-inch pieces
3 stalks celery, cut into 1-inch pieces
Hawaiian salt to taste
5 Tablespoons flour mixed with 5 tabbespoons water

Coat beef short ribs in flour and brown in oil in small batches. Place in large pot and add V8™ juice, beef broth and Tabasco™ sauce. Bring to a boil and simmer for 1 hour. Add carrots, potatoes, onion and celery. Add water if needed to cover ingredients. Bring to a boil and simmer for another 30 minutes or until vegetables are cooked. Add salt to taste, stir in flour mixture to desired thickness of gravy. (Add more if neccessary.)

Note: An original recipe shared by my sister-in-law that has been one of our favorite dishes at family gatherings. It is a hearty stew that not only tastes wonderful but is also a healthful dish.

Meatloaf

yield: 4 servings

2 pounds ground beef
2 eggs
1/2 cup bread crumbs
3/4 cup catsup
1/2 cup warm water
1 envelope onion soup mix (1-oz.)
1 can tomato sauce (8-oz.)

Combine all ingredients, except tomato sauce, and mix thoroughly. Put into a 9x5-inch loaf pan. Pour tomato sauce over all. Bake at 350°F for 1 hour.

Goulash

Quick and Easy

yield: 4 to 6 servings

1 pound ground beef
2 Tablespoons oil
1/2 onion, chopped
2 (8-oz.) cans tomato sauce
1 box frozen mixed vegetables (10-oz.)
salt and pepper to taste

Fry onion in hot oil; add beef. Cook, stirring, until light brown. Stir in tomato sauce and frozen vegetables. Simmer until vegetables are thawed and heated. Season with salt and pepper. Simmer for 5 minutes.

Oxtail Soup

yield: 4-6 servings

4 pounds oxtail, cut into pieces
2 cubes beef bouillon (Knorr™ brand, Extra Large Cubes)
2 cubes chicken bouillon (Knorr™ brand, Extra Large Cubes)
5 whole star anise
4 slivers ginger
1 cup shelled and skinned raw peanuts
Hawaiian salt to taste
Chinese parsley for garnish

Parboil oxtail 20 to 30 minutes. Rinse and trim fat. Place in a pot and cover with water approximately 2-inches above oxtail. Bring to a boil and add bouillon cubes, star anise and ginger. Simmer for 1 hour. Add peanuts. Simmer for another 1 to 1-1/2 hours, or until oxtail is tender. Skim off "scum" from broth. Add Hawaiian salt to taste. Garnish with Chinese parsley.

Variation: Serve with ground ginger and shoyu as a condiment.

Note: Shelled and skinned peanuts can be bought in Chinatown. Or you can shell and skin your own raw peanuts. Soak shelled peanuts in hot water to soften skin. Then remove. A definite local favorite! This recipe, shared by Florence Au, is not only easy to prepare but has the best-tasting broth which makes this recipe such a success with true oxtail lovers.

Easy Beef Stroganoff

yield: 4 servings

1 pound flank steak, thinly sliced
1/2 onion, chopped
1 clove garlic, minced
1/4 cup butter
2 teaspoons flour
1/2 teaspoon salt
1/4 teaspoon pepper
1 can mushrooms (6-oz.)
1 can cream of mushroom soup (10-3/4-oz.)
1/2 cup sour cream
1 package egg noodles (12-oz.)

Cook egg noodles according to package directions.

Sauté onions and garlic with butter. Add meat and simmer until tender. Add rest of ingredients and simmer 10 minutes. Pour over cooked noodles.

Note: I recommend this recipe for young cooks. It's delicious and so easy to prepare.

Barbecued Meat Balls

yield: 4 servings

1 pound ground beef
1/4 cup uncooked oatmeal
1 teaspoon salt
1/8 teaspoon pepper
1/3 cup milk (or less)
2 Tablespoons oil

Combine all ingredients (except oil) and mix well. Shape into balls. Brown meat balls in hot oil in a skillet and place browned meat balls in a saucepan.

Sauce:
1/2 cup catsup
2 Tablespoons vinegar
1 Tablespoon shoyu
2 Tablespoons brown sugar
1 Tablespoon Worcestershire™ sauce
2 teaspoons prepared mustard

Combine all ingredients for sauce and pour over meat balls. Cover and cook until meat balls are done (about 30 minutes).

Note: This is a favorite with children and teens. It's tasty and easy to prepare. When doubling the amount of meat balls, it's not necessary to double sauce.

DeLuz Vindha D'Ahlos Roast

yield: 3 to 4 servings

2 to 3 pounds roast (chuck or crossrib roast)
1 chili pepper (habaneros)
4 to 5 cloves garlic, crushed
1-1/2 Tablespoons Hawaiian salt
1/2 cup apple cider vinegar
1/2 cup water
2 potatoes, cut into large chunks
3 carrots, cut into large chunks
1 Portuguese sausage (5-oz.), sliced diagonally in 1-1/2"
lengths

Slice pepper lengthwise in three pieces. Mix pepper, garlic, salt and vinegar until salt dissolves. Rub on roast and marinate overnight in the refrigerator. Turn roast over a couple of times. When ready to cook, place roast with marinade liquid in a roasting pan. Add water, vegetables and sausage. Cover with foil and bake at 300°F for 2 hours. Uncover and bake for an additional 30 minutes or until done.

Note: The general rule is 1 hour roasting time per pound at 300°F. If roast is more or less than 3 pounds, adjust roasting time. This is a scaled-down version of Jackie DeLuz Watanabe's original recipe to accommodate smaller families. My neighbor, Darleen Dyer, has fond memories of her grandmother preparing vindha d'ahlos and liked this recipe.

Stuffed Cabbage Rolls

yield: 6 servings

1/2 pound ground beef
1/2 pound ground pork
3/4 cup cooked rice
1 egg, beaten
1/2 cup milk
1/4 cup onion, finely chopped
1 teaspoon Worcestershire™ sauce
3/4 teaspoon salt
dash of pepper
3 quarts water
12 cabbage leaves

Sauce:
1 can tomato soup (10-3/4-oz.)
1 Tablespoon brown sugar
1 Tablespoon lemon juice

In a bowl, combine pork, ground beef, rice, egg, milk, onion, Worcestershire™ sauce, salt and pepper; mix well. Boil 3 quarts water and immerse cabbage leaves about 3 minutes, or until limp; drain. Place about 1/4 cup meat mixture on each leaf; fold in sides. Starting at unfolded edge, roll up each leaf, making sure folded sides are included in roll. Arrange in a 12x7-1/2x2-inch baking dish.

Stir together sauce ingredients; pour over cabbage rolls. Bake, uncovered at 350°F for 1 hour and 15 minutes, basting once or twice with sauce.

Easy Pot Roast

yield: 6 to 8 servings

3 to 4 pounds 7-bone chuck roast
salt and pepper to season
2 Tablespoons oil
1 clove garlic, crushed
3 carrots, cut in 3-inch pieces
2 potatoes, quartered
2 onions, halved
1 can cream of mushroom soup (10-3/4-oz.)
1 envelope onion soup mix

Cut roast into 6 to 8 pieces (include bone in); season with salt and pepper. In large skillet, heat oil and brown garlic. Add roast pieces and brown on all sides. Lower heat. Spread cream of mushroom soup over roast pieces; sprinkle onion soup mix over that. Place carrots, potatoes and onions in a skillet. Cover and cook on low heat about 45 to 60 minutes, or until roast and vegetables are fork tender.

Note: This was often requested by the grandchildren for Grandma Watanabe to prepare her pot roast when they had dinner together.

Lasagne

yield: 8 to 10 servings

2 pounds hamburger

1 Tablespoon oil

1 clove garlic, minced

1 round onion, chopped

1 green pepper, chopped

1 can tomato sauce (15-oz.)

1 can tomato sauce (8-oz.)

2 teaspoons salt

2 cans (6-oz. each) "basil, garlic & oregano" tomato paste

3 cans water (measure with tomato paste can)

2 envelopes spaghetti sauce mix (1.37-oz. each)

1 box extra-wide lasagne noodles (16-oz.)

1 package mozzarella cheese slices (6-oz.)

Heat oil, brown garlic slightly. Add onion and green pepper and cook until tender. Add meat; do not overcook the meat. Add rest of ingredients (except noodles and mozzarella cheese slices) and simmer about 1 hour.

Cook noodles according to package directions. Rinse with cold water; drain.

Alternate layers of noodles and meat mixture in a 10x14-inch roasting pan, ending with meat mixture. Top with mozzarella cheese sheets. Bake at 325°F, uncovered, approximately 30 to 45 minutes or until cheese is lightly browned.

Optional: Add 1 container (16-oz.) cottage cheese, small curd, to layers.

Note: I sometimes use 2 Pyrex 7-1/2x11-3/4-inch pans. I can share one pan with relatives. My niece, Pat, especially enjoyed this lasagne, requesting no cottage cheese.

Hawaiian Teriyaki Burger

yield: 6 to 8 servings

1-1/2 pounds ground beef
1 small onion, chopped
1 egg
1/4 cup shoyu
1/4 cup sugar
2 cloves garlic, minced
1/2 teaspoon minced fresh ginger,
2 stalks green onion, chopped
1 Tablespoon sesame oil

Combine all ingredients; mix well. Form into patties. Fry, grill or broil.

Note: This is definitely a local favorite.

No-Fail Roast Beef

yield: 6 to 8 servings

Any size rib roast beef

Salt and pepper roast and let stand at room temperature for 1 hour. (Optional: poke holes here and there in the roast and put in little pieces of garlic.) Place beef, fat side up, in open roaster (not covered) and put in 350°F oven for 1 hour. Turn off heat but DO NOT OPEN DOOR AT ANY TIME UNTIL READY TO SERVE

For rare beef: 45 minutes before serving turn oven on to 300°F.
For medium beef: 50 minutes before serving, turn oven on to 300°F
For medium-well done beef: 55 minutes before serving, turn oven on to 300°F.

Note: Roast can be started in mid-afternoon or earlier. Allow at least 3 hours in the oven to complete cooking. Thanks to Janet Hirota and Ethel Nishida who shared this wonderful secret with the Puohala Elementary faculty and staff in 1975. It really is a no-fail recipe! I've been using it ever since then.

Chapche

yield: 4 servings

5 ounces lean beef, cut into julienne strips
1 bundle bean thread (1-3/4-oz.)
salt and pepper to taste
oil for frying

Beef marinade:
2 Tablespoons shoyu
1 Tablespoon sesame oil
1 teaspoon sugar
1 teaspoon sake or sherry
1/2 teaspoon mirin
2 cloves garlic, crushed

Bean thread marinade:
1 teaspoon roasted sesame seeds
2/3 teaspoon shoyu
1/2 teaspoon sugar
1/3 teaspoon sesame oil

Stir-fry vegetables:
4 dried shiitake mushrooms, soaked in water, sliced
1 small carrot, cut into julienne strips
1 small onion, cut into julienne strips
1 green pepper, cut into julienne strips

Marinate beef for 30 minutes.

Boil water and cook bean thread for 3 to 4 minutes until transparent. Remove and drain. Cut into 2-1/2-inch lengths. Combine bean thread marinade and mix well. Set aside.

Heat 2 Tablespoons oil and stir-fry vegetables and season with salt and pepper to taste. Set aside. In same pan, add a little oil and stir-fry beef and combine vegetables. Add bean thread to mixture and mix thoroughly. Transfer to a platter and serve.

· LAMB ·

Lamb Tips

- Select lamb that is pinkish-red and has a velvety texture.
- Lamb is lean and tender since it is marketed when it is about 6 to 8 months old.
- Lamb has little marbling and only a thin layer of fat around the outside of the meat.
- The thin, paper-like covering on the outer fat is called "fell." Trim the fell from steaks and chops for even cooking and appearance but keep it on roasts and legs because it helps to keep the shape and juiciness during cooking.
- Cook lamb to medium-rare (145°) or medium (160°) for best results.
- Roast at 325°F. Do not cover lamb when roasting.
- You may season lamb before, during or after cooking.
- For less tender cuts of lamb, marinate lamb before cooking.
- Marinate at least 6 hours to tenderize, but no longer than 24 hours.
- Slash outer edge of fat on lamb chops diagonally at 1″ intervals to prevent curling when cooking.
- To broil lamb, place on rack in foil-lined broiler pan.
- To check for doneness when grilling or broiling, cut a small slit in the center. Medium-rare is pink in the center and medium is light pink in color.

Herb Crusted Rack of Lamb

yield: 4 servings

2 (14 to 16-oz.) racks of lamb, fat trimmed
3 tablespoons Dijon mustard

Marinade:
2 Tablespoons rosemary
1 Tablespoon pepper or crushed peppercorns
1 teaspoon salt
2 Tablespoons olive oil
1 Tablespoon Worcestershire™ sauce
1/2 cup red wine
1/4 cup balsamic vinegar

Crust:
1/2 cup bread crumbs
1/4 cup chopped fresh parsley
2 cloves garlic, chopped
2 Tablespoons dried rosemary
2 Tablespoons dried thyme
olive oil to moisten

Combine marinade and rub over rack of lamb. Marinate overnight in the refrigerator.

Remove lamb from refrigerator and let set for 30 minutes at room temperature. In large skillet over medium-high heat, brown rack just to seal the outsides. Place in a roasting pan and rub with Dijon mustard. In a small bowl, combine crust ingredients and press crust mixture over loin of the rack. Cover the racks with foil to avoid burning. Roast in preheated oven at 325°F for 45 minutes or until done.

Lu-Bee (Green Beans With Lamb)

yield: 6 servings

1-1/2 pounds lamb, cut in cubes
3 Tablespoons olive oil
1 large onion, diced
3 to 4 cloves garlic, chopped
2 pounds green beans, cut in 2-inch lengths
1 teaspoon salt
1/2 teaspoon pepper
1 can Progresso™ "Italian Styled Peeled Tomatoes With Basil"
    (28-oz.)
2 cups water
1 Tablespoon fresh mint

Sauté lamb in oil. Add onions and garlic; cook until onions are tender. Add green beans, salt and pepper. Cover and cook on low heat 10 minutes or until beans turn bright green. Add rest of ingredients. Bring to a boil, lower heat and simmer for 1 hour.

Note: While shopping at Longs, I bumped into Stephanie Capllonch, mother of Maria and Theresa, my former students at Aikahi. She is of Lebanese descent and she shared this favorite lamb recipe. The fresh mint gives it a special flavor.

McCarthy's Marinade

yield: 3 to 5 servings

2 pounds lamb rib chops

Marinade:
1/4 cup olive oil
3 Tablespoons balsamic vinegar
6 to 7 cloves garlic, finely minced
1 Tablespoon thyme
1 teaspoon salt
1/4 teaspoon pepper

Combine ingredients and mix together. Place lamb rib chops in a plastic bag with marinade and seal. Marinate overnight. Grill over hibachi to preferred doneness.

Note: Liz McCarthy, mother of Stephanie M. (I also had Stephanie G. in my kindergarten class at Aikahi many years ago), gave me this favorite family marinade recipe while standing in line at a supermarket one day.

Lamb Stew With Peanuts

yield: 4 to 6 servings

1-1/2 pounds lamb stew meat or lean boneless lamb, cut into
   1-1/2-inch cubes
1-1/2 cups water
1 can stewed tomatoes (14-1/2-oz.)
1 small onion, sliced
1 stalk celery with leaves, chopped
1/4 cup chopped parsley
1 large clove garlic, crushed
1 cube beef bouillon
1 teaspoon salt
1/4 teaspoon ground thyme
1/8 teaspoon pepper
5 carrots, diced
6 small potatoes, quartered
1 teaspoon cornstarch mixed with 1 Tablespoon water
3/4 cup Planter's™ cocktail peanuts

Combine the first 11 ingredients in a large pot. Bring to a boil. Reduce heat to low, cover, and simmer for 1 hour and 30 minutes, or until lamb is tender. (Refrigerate to solidify fat.) Remove fat, bring to a boil and add carrots and potatoes. Reduce heat to low, cover, and simmer for 30 minutes or until vegetables are tender. Blend in cornstarch mixture to thicken stew. Stir in peanuts. Cover and cook for 5 minutes longer.

Variation: Peanuts may be left out. Lamb stew still tastes great.

Note: My husband preferred the stew without the peanuts. (But he also prefers ice cream without nuts or chips in them.)

Lamb Shish Kabob

yield: 4 servings

1 pound lamb, boneless shoulder, cut into 1-inch cubes
1 green pepper, cut into 1-inch pieces
1 medium onion, cut into eighths
1 cup eggplant, cubed

Marinade:
juice of one lemon (about 1/4 cup)
2 Tablespoons olive oil
2 teaspoons chopped fresh oregano leaves
   (or 1/2 teaspoon dried oregano leaves)
1-1/2 teaspoons salt
1/4 teaspoon pepper

Trim excess fat from lamb. Mix marinade ingredients. Stir in lamb until coated. Cover and refrigerate at least 6 hours.

Remove lamb from marinade; reserve marinade. Place vegetables in marinade and mix together. Let set 15 minutes. Thread lamb and vegetables on skewers, alternately, leaving space between each piece. Grill or broil, turning and brushing twice with any remaining marinade, until done.

Roast Lamb

yield: 6 to 8 servings

5 pounds boned rolled leg of lamb
salt and pepper to season
3 cloves garlic
2 (4-oz.) cans mushrooms, pieces and stems with liquid
2 to 3 round onions, chopped

Remove netting around rolled leg of lamb; unroll lamb. Prepare roast by rubbing salt and pepper all over. Slice garlic into slivers and poke into small gashes in surface of lamb. Fold over lamb and place, skin side up, in a foil-lined roasting pan. Roast, uncovered, at 325°F about 25 minutes per pound (or internal temperature of 165° F).

About 1 hour before roast is done, add onions and mushrooms. Continue roasting, basting with onion-mushroom sauce. Let roast set for 20 minutes before slicing. Serve with onion-mushroom sauce.

Optional: To make gravy, scoop out all onions and mushrooms. Make gravy with drippings, using cornstarch and chicken broth to thicken.

Note: I got this recipe from Jean Tanimoto, a former teacher at Puohala Elementary and a super cook! I love this roast lamb. Although retired, she is still preparing her delicious treats for the Puohala staff.

· PORK ·

Pork Tips

- Fresh pork should be grayish-pink in color and fine-grained in texture.
- Cook all pork to at least 160° (medium). For some cuts of pork, 170° (well done) is best to develop its flavor.
- Boneless pork cooked to medium done will be slightly pink in the center. Bone-in cuts will be a slightly brighter pink but both are safe to eat. Cut a slit in the center to check for doneness.
- The rainbow-like appearance on the surface of ham is safe and does not affect the quality of the ham.
- Check labels. "Fully cooked ham" is ready to eat without cooking. Ham labeled "Cook before eating" must be cooked to 160° to be safe.
- Country hams are specially flavored, cured and aged and are usually saltier than other hams.
- Roasting is a low-fat way to cook pork since the fat drips away from the roast while cooking. Not necessary to preheat oven.
- To roast, place pork, fat side up, on rack in foil-lined aluminum pan.
- Season and salt roast before cooking to enhance flavor.
- Roasts continue to cook after being removed from the oven. Do not cover roast tightly as it creates steam.
- Broiling and grilling are quick, low-fat methods for chops and other small pieces. Pan broiling is also a quick and low-fat way to cook thinner steaks and patties.

Lazy-Style Laulau

yield: 10 to 12 servings

8 ti leaves, rinsed and stiff rib removed
4 pounds taro (luau) leaves, rinsed and stems removed
3 pounds pork butt, cut into 1x1-inch chunks
1 to 2 pounds salted butterfish, cut into bite-size pieces
2 Tablespoons Hawaiian salt
1 cup water

Line a large roasting pan with foil. Lay 4 ti leaves in the pan, overlapping one over another. Use half of the luau leaves over the ti leaves. Arrange pork and fish evenly on leaves. Sprinkle with salt. Place remaining luau leaves on top. Pour water over all and cover with ti leaves on top. Cover pan tightly with foil. Bake at 350°F for 3 hours.

Variation: Sweet potatoes may be added before covering with ti leaves.

Southern Style Ribs

yield: 4 servings

2 to 4 pounds baby back ribs or pork rib racks
3 tablespoons brown sugar
1/2 teaspoon each: black pepper, chili powder, paprika
1/4 teaspoon Tabasco™
1/8 teaspoon cayenne pepper
1 Tablespoon finely minced garlic

Rinse and dry ribs. Cut into singles or doubles. Rub spices and sugar into ribs and knead well.

Sauce:
1 cup water
2 Tablespoons cider vinegar
1 Tablespoon Worcestershire™ sauce
juice of 1 large lemon
6 Tablespoons dark brown sugar
1-1/4 cups catsup
1/2 teaspoon each: paprika, celery seeds, chili powder, fresh grated ginger, Dijon mustard
3 drops Tabasco™
pinch of each: cayenne, coriander, cumin
salt and pepper to season
1 large onion, chopped
2 Tablespoons oil
1 clove garlic, minced

In a small bowl, mix all sauce ingredients except onion, oil and garlic. Stir until sugar melts. In a pot, sauté onion in oil until opaque, but not brown. Add garlic to onions; cook slightly. Then add sauce mixture and stir. Cook uncovered over low heat for 30 minutes, stirring occasionally.

Place ribs in a baking pan lined with 2 layers of foil. Cover with more foil and seal. Cook a 400°F for 40 minutes. Open foil carefully to release steam. Remove ribs to a large bowl. Discard fat and used foil.

Dip ribs in sauce and return to pan. Bake uncovered at 450°F for 5 to 7 minutes until a crust begins to form. Dip in sauce again and return to oven for another 5 to 7 minutes.

Note: This is not as difficult to do as it may appear. You need to stock up on more spices, but once you taste these "finger-licking" ribs, you'll want to cook this again.

Kau Yuk (Steamed Red Pork)

yield: 8 to 10 servings

3 pounds belly pork
1 pound taro, sliced 1/2-inch thick
oil for frying

Heat oil and brown sliced taro. Set aside. Parboil belly pork for 15 minutes. Rinse and paper towel dry. Puncture skin with knife or fork. Heat oil in a heavy pot and fry skin side down until brown and crisp. Remove from the pot and cool. Cut into slices, approximately 1x4-inches. Arrange in large bowl, alternating taro and pork slices.

Sauce:
    1 bottle red bean curd sauce (8-oz.)
    3 Tablespoons brown sugar
    1 teaspoon Hawaiian salt
    2 Tablespoons hoisin sauce
    2 Tablespoons oyster sauce
    1/2 teaspoon five spices
    2 cloves garlic, minced
    1 whole star anise (mashed)
    1 Tablespoon sherry

Mix all ingredients. Pour over meat and taro in a bowl. Marinate for 2 hours or overnight. Steam for 2-1/2 hours.

Laulau

yield: 12 laulaus

1 pound pork, cut in 1x1-inch chunks
1 pound brisket stew meat, cut in 1x1-inch chunks
3/4 pound salted butterfish, cut in small pieces
3 pounds taro (luau) leaves, washed and stems removed
24 ti leaves, washed and stiff rib removed
Hawaiian salt to season

Divide pork, meat and fish into 12 parts. Salt pork and meat to taste. Wrap a piece of pork, meat and fish in 8 to 10 taro leaves.

Place the wrapped bundle (laulau) in the center of a ti leaf and wrap the ti leaf around the laulau. Use a second ti leaf and wrap around the laulau in the opposite direction, making a flat package. Tie securely with string. Place wrapped laulaus in steamer and steam, covered, 4 hours or longer.

Variation: Substitute pork and meat with skinless chicken thighs.

Tonkatsu

yield: 5 servings

5 pork cutlets
oil for browning
salt, pepper and garlic salt to season
1/2 cup flour for coating
1/2 cup bread crumbs
1 egg, beaten

Sauce:
1/2 cup catsup
1 teaspoon dry mustard
1 Tablespoon water
2 Tablespoons Worcestershire™ sauce
1/2 teaspoon Tabasco™ sauce

Pound pork cutlets and season with salt, pepper and garlic salt. Let set for 15 minutes. Dredge pork cutlets in flour, dip in egg and roll in bread crumbs. Heat oil and cook until golden brown. Drain on paper towel. Slice into 1-inch strips. Combine sauce and serve with cutlets.

Sari Sari

yield: 4 to 5 servings

1/2 pound Chinese roast pork
1 Tablespoon oil
3 cloves garlic, crushed
1/2 round onion, wedged
1 tomato, wedged
1 teaspoon salt, or to taste
1 cup water or chicken broth
2 long-type eggplants, halved lengthwise and cut in 1-inch
   slices
1/2 pound string beans, cut into thirds
1 long squash, peeled, cut into chunks (or 1/2 pumpkin)

Heat oil in a pot. Brown garlic, onion and tomato. Add pork, season with salt and cook 5 minutes. Add water or chicken broth and bring to a boil. Add vegetables and cook until vegetables are tender.

Variation: Substitute pork with 18 medium-size shrimp (31-40 count), peeled and cleaned. Add shrimp when squash is almost done.

Aburage Stuffed With Pork Hash

yield: 32 pieces

1-1/2 pounds ground pork
6 to 8 ounces Chinese fishcake, uncooked
1 Tablespoon rinsed and minced chung choy
3 to 4 shiitake mushrooms, soaked and finely chopped
6 to 8 water chestnuts, minced
2 to 3 stalks green onion, finely chopped
2 Tablespoons oyster sauce
1 Tablespoon shoyu
1/2 teaspoon salt
2 packages small size aburage (8 aburage per package)
    (2-oz. each), 16 pieces total

Mix all ingredients (except aburage) in a medium bowl. Cut aburage in half into triangles. Stuff aburage with pork mixture. Place in a bowl and steam 35 to 40 minutes. Serve with shoyu and mustard sauce or with gravy. (See recipe below.)

Gravy:
    1-1/2 cup chicken broth
    1 Tablespoon oyster sauce
    1 Tablespoon shoyu
    1 teaspoon sesame oil
    salt to season (optional)
    2 Tablespoons cornstarch mixed with 2 Tablespoons
        water

Mix all gravy ingredients (except cornstarch mixture) in a small saucepan and bring to a boil. Stir in cornstarch mixture to thicken and simmer until done. Pour over stuffed aburage.

Baked Spam™

yield: 4 to 6 pieces

2 cans Spam™ (12-oz. each)
1/2 cup brown sugar
1 can crushed pineapple (8-oz.)
whole cloves

Lay Spam™ flat in a baking pan. Stud Spam™ with cloves. Top with sugar and pineapple. Bake at 350°F for 30 minutes.

Variation: Place canned yams around meat the last 10 minutes of baking.

Pork Adobo

yield: 5 to 6 servings

4 to 5 pounds pork butt, cut in 1-inch cubes
5 cloves garlic, crushed
1 cup vinegar
1 to 2 bay leaves (optional)
salt and pepper to season

Combine ingredients in a large pot and marinate overnight, turning every 3 hours. Bring to a boil, then simmer on medium-low heat for about 1 hour. Turn occasionally.

Black Bean Spareribs

yield: 3 to 4 servings

3 pounds pork spareribs
flour for coating
oil for browning spareribs

Black bean mixture:
2 Tablespoons rinsed and mashed black beans (dau see)
3 cloves garlic, minced
2 Tablespoons shoyu
2 Tablespoons oyster sauce
1 Tablespoon sugar

Broth mixture:
1 can chicken broth (12-oz.)
1 cup water
1 cube chicken bouillon
1/4 cup cornstarch mixed with 1/4 cup water

Rinse ribs and drain well. Dredge in flour lightly. Heat oil and brown ribs. Add black bean mixture while browning. Add broth mixture (except for cornstarch mixed with 1/4 cup water) and bring to a boil. Stir in cornstarch mixed with water to thicken. Cover and simmer for 45 minutes.

Note: A local favorite that is popular in Chinese restaurants. This recipe is so tasty that it can stand up to any restaurant's recipe.

Sweet Sour Spareribs

yield: 4 to 6 servings

3 pounds spareribs
1/2 cup flour for coating
3 Tablespoons oil for browning ribs
3/4 cup brown sugar
1 cup water
1 Tablespoon salt
1/2 cup cider vinegar
4 Tablespoons sugar
3 cloves garlic, finely minced

Coat ribs with flour and brown ribs in hot oil. Drain oil. Mix rest of the ingredients and add to ribs. Simmer ribs for 2 hours, or until soft. Stir to prevent sticking.

Variation: Add sliced daikon and carrots to spareribs a few minutes before serving.

Note: Spareribs may be cooked the day before, refrigerated and fat removed the next day before serving. My neighbor, Audrey, got this recipe from her sister-in-law, Ella.

Stuffed Bitter Melon

yield: 4 to 6 pieces

5 bitter melons (about 2-1/2 pounds)
oil for frying
1 Tablespoon rinsed and mashed salted black beans
1 clove garlic, crushed

Filling:
1 pound lean ground pork
3 to 4 shiitake mushrooms, soaked and finely chopped
6 water chestnuts, minced
1 stalk green onion, thinly sliced
1/2 teaspoon salt
1/4 teaspoon sugar
2 teaspoons shoyu
dash of pepper
1 Tablespoon cornstarch

Gravy:
1 can chicken broth (14-1/2-oz.)
1 Tablespoon oyster sauce
2 teaspoons shoyu
1/2 teaspoon sugar
3 Tablespoons cornstarch mixed with 3 tablespoons water

Cut bitter melons into 1-inch lengths and remove centers. Parboil melons in water until slightly softened; drain. Combine filling ingredients. Fill melons with pork mixture.

Prepare a large pot for stuffed bitter melon. Heat 1 tablespoon oil and sauté black beans and garlic. (Do not burn garlic and black beans.) Turn off heat and set aside.

In a frying pan, heat 2 tablespoons oil on medium heat and brown both ends of stuffed melons. Remove and place in prepared pot with black beans and garlic. Brown another batch. Repeat until all are browned. (If any pork mixture is left, form into balls, brown and add to pot.) Carefully turn over bitter melon to coat black bean all over. Cover pot, turn to medium-high until hot, then turn heat to medium-low. Steam-cook for about 30 minutes, or until done. Carefully turn over occasionally.

Remove bitter melons. Combine sauce ingredients (except cornstarch mixture) and bring to a boil. Thicken with cornstarch mixture. Return bitter melons to the pot. Cook for an additional 10 minutes on low heat.

Note: This is another of Jennifer's requests when she comes home from Atlanta. If you like bitter melon, this dish is the best! I tried to make the steps easy to follow.

Barbecue Pork Ribs

yield: 4 to 6 servings

4 pounds pork ribs (slab)
1/4 cup vinegar

Seasoning Spices:
salt and pepper to season
paprika to taste
garlic salt to taste

Marinade:
1 bottle barbecue sauce (18-oz.), select your favorite
sauce
1/2 cup orange marmalade
2 Tablespoons oyster sauce
2 Tablespoons hoisin sauce
2 Tablespoons shoyu

Place ribs in a large pot. Cover ribs with water and add vinegar. Boil for 1-1/2 to 2 hours, or until tender. Remove from the pot; cool. Sprinkle seasoning spices on both sides of slab. Place in a sealable plastic bag and add marinade sauce in the bag. Marinate ribs for 4 hours or overnight. Place ribs on grill for 15 minutes before serving.

Note: An original recipe shared by Diane Au. It combines some of the local sauces with the traditional BBQ sauce ingredients to produce a unique and tasty dish. This recipe is so good that it has become her signature dish at family gatherings.

Oven Kalua Pig

yield: 6 servings

4 to 6-pounds pork butt
2 to 3 Tablespoons Hawaiian salt
2 Tablespoons liquid smoke
16 ti leaves (more or less depending on ti leaf size)
string for tying

Cut off ti leaf stems, remove stiff rib and wash leaves. Arrange leaves in a circular pattern, overlapping leaves.

Score pork butt all over and place in a container. Rub all sides of pork butt with salt and liquid smoke. Place butt, fat side up, on ti leaves. Wrap butt with ti leaves to completely cover and tie securely with string. Place the wrapped butt on heavy aluminum foil and seal well so no steam escapes. Place the prepared butt in a shallow roasting pan and roast in a preheated 450°F oven. After 1 hour, reduce heat to 400°F and cook 3 to 4 hours longer or until done. Shred and add more Hawaiian salt to taste, if desired.

Note: It tastes like the real thing!

Teri Pork Chops

yield: 2 servings

4 pork chops
2 Tablespoons oil for frying
3 Tablespoons shoyu
4 teaspoons sugar
1 small chili pepper, seeded and thinly sliced
   (or 1/4 teaspoon crushed red pepper)

Marinade:
2 Tablespoons shoyu
2 Tablespoons mirin
3 Tablespoons oil
2 cloves garlic, minced
1/2 teaspoon grated fresh ginger

Combine marinade ingredients and marinate pork chops for 15 minutes. In a large skillet heat 2 tablespoons oil over medium-high heat and brown pork chops on both sides. Lower to medium heat and cook pork chops until done, about 5 to 6 minutes. Add soy sauce, sugar and chili pepper and stir well until sugar is dissolved and pork chops are coated.

Spicy Eggplant With Pork

yield: 2 servings

2 teaspoons minced fresh ginger

2 teaspoons minced garlic

3 Tablespoons shoyu

2 teaspoons sugar

2 teaspoons vinegar

1/2 fresh red chili pepper, smashed, or 1/4 teaspoon crushed
red pepper

1 teaspoon cornstarch

1 large round eggplant, cut into 1-inch long strips

1/2 cup ground pork

1 cup oil

Mix together ginger, garlic, shoyu, sugar, vinegar, chili pepper, and cornstarch. Set aside. Heat oil in a frying pan until hot. Add eggplant and fry in oil until pulp is tender. Place eggplant pieces between paper towels and press lightly to remove excess oil. Add pork to the pan and cook; then remove pork and pour out oil. Heat the sauce in the pan until near boiling. Add the eggplant and pork. Mix together until thoroughly heated. Add a little water if too dry. Serve over hot rice.

Note: This is my friend, Nancy Weisner's, very tasty dish. If you like eggplant, this is a wonderful, hot and spicy dish. Be sure to serve it with hot rice.

Tired Teacher's Dinner

yield: 6 to 8 servings

3 pounds meat (pork butt cut into large chunks, short ribs, or chicken)
1 can tomato sauce (8-oz.)
1 can sugar (use tomato sauce can)
1 can shoyu (use tomato sauce can)
3 cloves garlic, crushed
1-inch piece fresh ginger, crushed
salt and pepper to season
whiskey to taste (optional)

Pour tomato sauce in a pot. Fill can with sugar and add to the pot. Add shoyu, garlic, ginger and seasonings. Place meat in sauce and cook, covered, on low to moderate heat for about 40 to 60 minutes, or until tender.

Note: Also known as "Dutch Oven Pork Roast" and "One Can Pork Roast"

Pork Hash

yield: 2 to 4 servings

1 pound ground pork

1 teaspoon salt

1 teaspoon cornstarch

1/2 teaspoon sugar

1 teaspoon sherry

1 teaspoon sesame oil

1 Tablespoon shoyu

1 Tablespoon oyster sauce

1 egg

1 Tablespoon soaked and diced chung choy

4 dried mushrooms, soaked and diced

1/2 cup minced water chestnuts (optional)

2 Tablespoons thinly sliced green onion (optional)

Combine all ingredients and mix well. Place in a large bowl or platter and flatten. Steam for 45 minutes.

Harm Ha Pork

yield: 3 to 4 servings

1 pound belly pork, cut in bite-size pieces

Seasoning:
   1 teaspoon harm ha (shrimp sauce)
   1/2 teaspoon sugar
   1 Tablespoon shoyu
   1 Tablespoon oyster sauce

Combine seasoning ingredients and coat belly pork with seasoning. Place in a bowl and steam for 1 hour.

Roast Pork

yield: 8 servings

3 pounds pork butt
salt, pepper and garlic salt to season

Place pork butt on foil-lined 9x13-inch pan. Season with salt, pepper and garlic salt. Preheat oven to 350°F and bake for 35 minutes per pound. Slice roast pork 1/4″ thick and serve with your favorite gravy.

Note: An everyday local favorite that is so easy to prepare!

Pork-Tofu Casserole

yield: 6 to 8 servings

1 pound lean ground pork
1 teaspoon oil
8 dried mushrooms, soaked and sliced
1 onion, sliced
1 can water chestnuts (8-oz.), drained and chopped
2 Tablespoons sake
1/4 teaspoon salt
1/4 cup shoyu
2 Tablespoons sugar
1 block firm tofu (20-oz.), cut into 1-inch cubes
2 large eggs, beaten
2 stalks green onion, chopped

Fry pork in oil; add mushrooms, onions and water chestnuts; sauté until pork is browned. Add sake, salt, shoyu and sugar; stir to mix well. Place tofu cubes in bottom of a 3-quart glass casserole dish or 9x13-inch pan sprayed with vegetable spray. Pour pork mixture over tofu. Pour eggs evenly over pork mixture. Sprinkle green onion over. Cover with foil and bake at 350°F for 35 minutes.

Variation: Substitute pork with ground turkey. Add 1/4 cup bamboo shoots, sliced, with the mushrooms and onions.

Pig's Feet

yield: 4 servings

5 pig's feet, legs
1-1/2 pounds ginger, 3-inch lengths
3 to 4 teaspoons Hawaiian salt
1/2 gallon vinegar
1/2 gallon water
1 bottle black vinegar (21-oz.)
1 bottle water (use black vinegar bottle)
3 packages Chinese block brown sugar (5-oz. each)

Parboil pig's feet for 15 to 20 minutes. Clean hair off legs with a sharp knife, at the same time rinsing off "scum" on pig's feet.

Soak ginger in water for 30 minutes to soften skin. Peel, slice in half lengthwise and smash. Marinate with Hawaiian salt for 6 hours or overnight.

Boil vinegar, 1/2 gallon water, black vinegar and the water in the black vinegar bottle. Add ginger and cook until ginger is soft. Add sugar to taste; bring to a boil. Add pig's feet; bring to a boil. Continue boiling until pig's feet are cooked, about 45 minutes to 1 hour.

Note: An original family recipe and now shared for the first time by Edward Au. In Chinese tradition, this dish was prepared to celebrate a new birth in the family and given to close family and friends. This recipe was so "onolicious" that Mr. Au was getting many requests to prepare this dish more often throughout the year.

Ma Po Tofu (Pork Tofu)

yield: 2 to 3 servings

1/4 pound pork hash
2 Tablespoons oil
1/8 cup dried soaked shrimps
1/2 cup chicken broth
1 block firm tofu (20-oz.), cut into 1x 2-inch cubes
1 stalk green onion, finely cut for garnish
Chinese parsley, cut in 1-inch lengths for garnish

Sauce:
2 Tablespoons cornstarch
2 Tablespoons water
2 Tablespoons shoyu
1 Tablespoon oyster sauce
1 teaspoon Hawaiian salt
1 teaspoon chili garlic sauce

Heat oil; sauté pork hash and dried shrimps. Add broth. Bring to a boil; simmer, covered, for 5 minutes. Add tofu and stir lightly until well heated. Add sauce mixture and heat until thickened. Garnish.

Mushroom Pork Chops

yield: 3 to 4 servings

6 pork chops
oil for browning
salt, pepper, garlic salt to season
1 can cream of mushroom soup (10-3/4-oz.)
1-1/2 cups milk

Season pork chops with salt, pepper and garlic salt. Heat oil and brown pork chops. Place in a foil-lined 9x13-inch pan. Combine soup with milk. Pour mixture over pork chops. Place in preheated 350°F oven and bake for 1 hour.

Note: A quick and easy favorite for the busy family during the weekdays.

Okinawa-Style Pork

yield: 8 to 10 servings

3 to 4 pounds pork butt
2 cloves garlic, crushed
2-inch ginger root, sliced
water to cover pork
1 cup pork stock
1/4 cup mirin
1/2 cup shoyu
1 cup sake or whiskey
1/3 cup sugar

Bring pork, garlic, ginger and water to a boil in covered pot. Uncover and skim off "scum" that forms. Cover, adjust heat and simmer for 30 to 40 minutes. Remove pork; drain, reserving 1 cup of liquid. Cool pork and slice into 2-inch squares. Combine 1 cup of preceding stock, mirin, shoyu, sake and sugar in the same pot. Lay pork squares in sauce and cook, covered, for 1-1/2 hours over low heat. Uncover and continue cooking for 1/2 hour, turning pieces to glaze.

Pineapple Ribs

yield: 4 to 6 servings

3 to 4 pounds pork spareribs or baby back ribs, chopped
in 2-1/2-inch lengths
3 Tablespoons oil for frying
1 can pineapple chunks (15-oz.), drained

Marinade:
1-1/2 teaspoons Hawaiian salt
1/2 teaspoon pepper
1-1/2 Tablespoons cornstarch
1 teaspoon sugar
1 Tablespoon oil

Sauce:
1 cup Chinese vinegar or balsamic vinegar
1/3 cup apple cider vinegar
4-1/2 Tablespoons brown sugar (or 3 cubes Chinese
brown sugar)
1/4 cup fresh thin ginger slices
1/4 Tablespoon salt

Rinse ribs and pat dry with paper towel. Cut into singles. Marinate ribs in
marinade for 30 minutes. Then heat 3 tablespoons oil for frying. Put a batch
of ribs in a pan. Brown both sides, remove and place in a large pot. Add another batch to brown. Repeat until all ribs are browned.

Place sauce into the pot with ribs. Bring to a boil, lower heat to medium-low
and cook, uncovered, for about 1 hour and 15 minutes, or until almost dry. Stir
occasionally. Mix in pineapple chunks.

*Note: Ginger slices are edible and delicious. If there are any leftovers, ribs may
be frozen.*

Oxtail Soup (p.25)

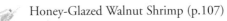

Honey-Glazed Walnut Shrimp (p.107)

Laulau (p.49), Lomi Salmon (p.123)
and Chicken Long Rice (p.83)

 Tripe Stew (p.142)

Kalbi (p.19) and Chapche (p.34)

 DeLuz Vindha D'Ahlos Roast (p.28)

 Hamburger Steak With Gravy, "Loco Moco" style (p.10)

Mochiko Chicken (p.93)

Pig's Feet (p.66)

Nishime (p.139)

Curried Lobster With Fried Haupia (p.120)

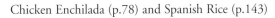 Cold Chicken With Ginger Sauce (p.87)

Chicken Enchilada (p.78) and Spanish Rice (p.143)

 Gon Lo Mein (p.137)

· POULTRY ·

Chicken Cacciatore

yield: 4 servings

2 pounds chicken thighs, skinless and boneless
1 cup flour
1 teaspoon salt
1 teaspoon black pepper
1 teaspoon paprika
olive oil for frying
1 onion, thinly sliced in rings or half circles
1 large can tomato sauce (15-oz.)
1 large can whole tomatoes (28-oz.)
1 to 2 green peppers, wedged
2 bay leaves
2 teaspoons oregano

Combine flour, salt, pepper and paprika in a bowl. Coat chicken in flour mixture. In a large, deep skillet, add enough olive oil to brown onions; remove onions. Add more oil as needed and cook floured chicken until golden brown and cooked through. Return onions to the pan. Add rest of the ingredients. Simmer, covered, for 1 to 2 hours.

Suggestion: Serve over hot linguine or hot rice.

Note: Whole chicken, or other chicken pieces, may be substituted. This is the best "Chicken Cacciatore" recipe I've found. It's full-flavored and very tomato sauce rich.

Cashew Chicken

yield: 4 to 6 servings

1-1/2 pounds boneless chicken, cut into 1 inch cubes
1 cup cashews
3 stalks celery, cut into 1-inch cubes
2 carrots, cut into 1/2-inch cubes, microwave 2 minutes
1 green pepper, cut into 1-inch cubes
1 onion, cut into 1-inch cubes
oil for frying

Seasoning:
1/2 teaspoon salt
1/2 teaspoon sugar
1/2 teaspoon pepper
1 Tablespoon sesame oil
1 Tablespoon oil
1 egg white

Combine seasoning ingredients; marinate chicken with seasoning and refrigerate for 2 hours. Heat oil in a skillet and brown chicken. Remove chicken. Stir-fry vegetables until crisp tender; add chicken and cashews. Toss together.

Note: My sister in-law's (Amy) family recipe. One of the best cashew chicken recipes that I have tasted and is also a healthy dish for the family.

Five Spices Shoyu Chicken

yield: 6 servings

3 to 4 pounds chicken
1/2 cup shoyu
1/2 cup water
2 teaspoons sugar
1 teaspoon oyster sauce
1 clove garlic, crushed
1-inch piece fresh ginger, grated
dash of 5 spices

Bring to a boil all ingredients (except chicken.) Add chicken to mixture and bring to a boil again. Lower heat and simmer 40 to 45 minutes, or until chicken is tender.

Serving Suggestion:
Parboil 3 cups of Chinese cabbage cut into 1-1/2-inch lengths. Drain and place on a serving platter. Place cooked chicken on Chinese cabbage. Add 3 Tablespoons cornstarch mixed with 3 Tablespoons water to sauce to thicken. Pour over chicken and garnish with Chinese parsley.

Note: Ruby Saito's mother makes this shoyu chicken with less sugar than other recipes.

Chicken Chili

yield: 10 to 12 servings

2 pounds ground chicken
2 Tablespoons oil
2 onions, diced
4 cloves garlic, minced
2 cans red kidney beans (14-1/2-oz. each)
1 can diced stewed tomatoes (14-1/2-oz.)
2 cans tomato sauce (8-oz. each)
5 Tablespoons chili powder
2 teaspoons garlic salt
2 teaspoons oregano
2 teaspoons cumin
2 teaspoons black pepper

Heat oil and brown chicken in a large pot. Add onions and garlic and cook, covered, until onions are soft. Add all other ingredients and simmer, covered, on low heat for 2 hours, stirring occasionally.

Note: For spicier chili, add 1 teaspoon crushed red pepper and 1/2 teaspoon cayenne pepper.

Chicken Enchilada

yield: 8 to 10 enchiladas

3 to 4 pounds chicken thighs, skinless and boneless
1 medium onion, diced
salt to season
2 packages cream cheese (8-oz. each)
1/2 pint whipping cream
1 package flour tortilla, 10 count (16-oz.)
1 can Las Palmas™ green chili enchilada sauce (19-oz.)
2 to 3 cups shredded cheddar cheese
salsa for topping (select your favorite salsa)

Boil chicken and shred; place in a large bowl. Add onion and sprinkle salt to taste. In a separate bowl, combine cream cheese and whipping cream. Mix until smooth. Add to chicken and onion; mix together. Place filling onto each tortilla and roll up. Place on greased 9x13-inch pan. (8 to 10 rolls should fit, depending on thickness of rolls.) Pour enchilada sauce over and sprinkle cheese on top. Bake at 350°F for 30 minutes. Serve with salsa.

Note: My niece, Donna Watanabe, introduced me to this great-tasting enchilada. I shared it with my neighbor, who then shared it at a potluck. It's very rich, so I usually cut each piece in half.

Black Bean Chicken With Lup Cheong

yield: 4 to 6 servings

6 pieces chicken thighs, boneless and skinless, chopped
1 tablespoon sesame oil
3 pieces lup cheong, sliced thinly
1 large onion, chopped
3 cloves garlic, crushed
1 tray fresh mushrooms (8-oz.), sliced
1 cup chopped green onion
2 teaspoons Lee Kum Kee™ black bean garlic sauce
1 to 2 teaspoons sugar

Fry onion in sesame oil. Add chopped pieces of chicken; cook until chicken is almost done. Add lup cheong and garlic and stir-fry. Add mushrooms, green onions, black bean garlic sauce and sugar. Cook until mushrooms are done.

Note: From Maui, Glennis Ooka shared this unique and tasty dish.

Chicken Adobo

yield: 6 to 8 servings

3 pounds chicken thighs, skinless, cut in half with bone in

1/2 cup white vinegar

1/2 cup shoyu

1 teaspoon brown sugar

2 Tablespoons peppercorns, crush about half

5 cloves garlic, crushed

3 bay leaves

salt to season

Combine all ingredients in a pan; cover and marinate 1 to 3 hours. Bring to a boil, then lower heat and simmer for 30 minutes. Remove cover and simmer for an additional 15 minutes, or until most of the liquid has evaporated and the chicken is lightly brown.

Note: This is the best chicken adobo I've ever tasted.

Chicken Katsu

yield: 6 servings

2 pounds chicken breasts, boneless and skinless
garlic salt to season
1/2 cup flour
2 eggs, beaten
2 cups panko flakes (flour meal for breading)
oil for frying

Katsu sauce:
1/3 cup catsup
1/4 cup shoyu
1/4 cup sugar
1-1/2 teaspoons Worcestershire™ sauce
pinch of ground red pepper

Combine all katsu sauce ingredients; mix well. Set aside.

Season chicken generously with garlic salt and let stand 15 to 30 minutes. Heat about 1/2 inch of oil in a skillet. Dredge chicken in flour, dip in eggs and coat with panko in that order. Fry chicken until golden brown on both sides; drain on paper towels. Cut into 1-inch slices. Serve with katsu sauce.

Note: This is so-o-o good! The chicken is tender inside and light and crispy on the outside. Kristen Hasegawa's favorite!

Italian Chicken

yield: 6 to 8 servings

2 to 3 pounds chicken thighs, skinless and boneless

1/2 cup flour

1/4 cup olive oil

2 jars marinated artichokes (6-oz. each), with liquid

2 cans whole tomatoes (14-1/2-oz. each), drained

4 cloves garlic, minced

1 large tray fresh mushrooms (14-oz.), sliced

1 cup sherry

1-1/2 teaspoons salt

1/4 teaspoon pepper

1 teaspoon oregano

2 teaspoons basil

Lightly flour chicken; brown in hot olive oil and add all the liquid from artichoke jars (reserve artichokes for later.) Simmer, covered, for 5 to 10 minutes. Place chicken in a casserole dish or lightly greased 9x13-inch pan. In a large bowl, mix together remaining ingredients (except artichokes) and pour over chicken. Bake, uncovered, at 350°F for 50 minutes. Add artichokes and bake for an additional 10 minutes.

Note: Do try this. It's delicious!

Cold Chicken With Ginger Sauce

yield: 4-6 servings

2 quarts water
1 Tablespoon salt
1-inch piece ginger
4 pounds frying or roasting chicken
Chinese parsley, chopped (optional)

Ginger Sauce:
1 Tablespoon Hawaiian salt
1 clove garlic, finely minced
1/3 cup finely minced ginger
1/3 cup minced green onion
1/2 cup salad oil

Boil water, salt and 1-inch piece ginger. Add whole chicken, cover and immediately turn to lowest heat for 30 minutes. Turn chicken over; cover the pot for another 30 minutes at lowest heat. Remove chicken and rinse quickly with cold water or let sit in cold water until chicken is cool. Drain and refrigerate. Cut chicken in 2x1-inch pieces and place in a serving dish. Place in the refrigerator to chill.

In a small bowl, combine salt, garlic, ginger and green onion. Heat oil and pour over green onion mixture; mix well. Pour sauce over chicken pieces. Garnish with parsley, if desired.

Note: Chicken must be fresh and not frozen for best results.

Easy Curry For Two

yield: 2 servings

2 chicken thighs, deboned and skinless, cut into bite-size
   pieces
1 can of cream of mushroom soup (10-3/4-oz.)
2 Tablespoons water
curry mix pieces (i.e., S&B Golden Curry™)

Heat cream of mushroom soup with 2 Tablespoons water. Break off a small piece from the curry mix and blend with soup. Taste and add more pieces as desired. Heat to boiling, add chicken and simmer for about 15 to 20 minutes, or until chicken is tender and done.

Variation: Substitute chicken with shrimp. Add frozen or canned vegetables.

Note: Select mild, medium or hot curry. Many brands are available. My nephew, Craig Kutsunai, gave me this recipe. His sister, Chris, likes it because it's easy to prepare and it's also very tasty.

Baked Chicken and Stuffing

yield: 6 servings

6 skinless, boneless chicken breast halves or thighs
1 package instant chicken-flavored stuffing mix (6-oz.)
1 can cream of chicken soup (10-3/4-oz.)
1/3 cup milk
1 Tablespoon chopped fresh parsley
paprika for sprinkling

Prepare stuffing mix according to package directions, but do not let stand as directed. Spoon stuffing, crosswise, in the center of a 9x13-inch inch pan, leaving space on both sides of stuffing to arrange chicken. Arrange 3 chicken pieces on each side of stuffing, overlapping, if necessary.

In a bowl, combine soup, milk and parsley. Pour over chicken. Cover with foil; bake at 400° for 15 minutes. Uncover, bake 10 minutes more or until chicken is no longer pink.

To serve, sprinkle with paprika. Stir sauce at edges and spoon over chicken.

Turkey Divan

yield: 2 to 3 servings

1 bunch broccoli, chopped into bite-size pieces
2 cups shredded cooked turkey
1 can cream of mushroom soup (10-3/4-oz.)

Place broccoli in a casserole dish and cook in the microwave until slightly undercooked. Place shredded turkey over broccoli. Pour cream of mushroom soup over turkey and cook in the microwave about 4 minutes on high. Mix before serving.

Variation: Substitute turkey with "huli huli" chicken.

Note: Great for left-over turkey!

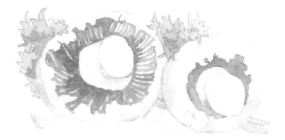

Mushroom Chicken

yield: 4 to 6 servings

2 to 3 pounds chicken pieces
1 clove garlic, minced
salt and pepper to season
flour for dredging
3 Tablespoons oil
1 can cream of mushroom soup (10-3/4-oz.)
3/4 can water (use soup can)
1 tray fresh mushrooms (8-oz.), sliced

Rinse chicken pieces and pat dry. Rub garlic, salt and pepper all over chicken pieces. Dredge in flour and fry in heated oil. Add cream of mushroom soup and water. Simmer for approximately 15 minutes. Add mushrooms and simmer for another 5 to 10 minutes.

Oven-Fried Chicken

yield: 4 to 6 servings

2 to 3 pounds boneless chicken breasts or thighs
1/2 cup mayonnaise
1-1/2 teaspoons salt
pepper to season
1/4 teaspoon garlic salt
1 cup crushed corn flakes

Rinse and dry chicken. Combine mayonnaise, salt, pepper and garlic salt. Coat chicken with mixture; roll in crushed corn flakes. Place in a foil-lined 9x13-inch pan. Bake at 400°F for 25 minutes; then lower temperature to 350°F and bake for an additional 20 minutes.

Easy Roast Chicken

yield: 2 to 4 servings

2-3 pounds fryer
Hawaiian salt to season
1 clove garlic, grated

Rinse fryer and pat dry. Rub Hawaiian salt (and garlic, if desired) in cavity and all over chicken. Place in a pan or corningware. Bake at 400°F for 1 hour.

Note: At Aikahi Elementary, this is known as "Lorna's chicken" because Lorna Tam Ho shared how she did her roast chicken.

Cantonese Shoyu Chicken

yield: 6 to 8 servings

5 pounds chicken thighs, skinless
1/2 cup shoyu
2 Tablespoons honey
1/2 cup brown sugar
1-1/2 cups water
2-inch piece ginger, sliced
2 to 3 cloves garlic, crushed
2 to 3 stalks green onion, cut into 2-1/2-inch lengths
2 Tablespoons cornstarch mixed with 2 Tablespoons water

In a large pot, add all ingredients (except green onion) and bring to a boil. Add green onion, cover, and simmer for 30 minutes. Remove chicken from the pot; arrange on a platter. Bring liquid to a boil and skim off fat. Add cornstarch mixture to sauce and cook, stirring briskly, until thickened. Pour over chicken and serve.

Serving suggestion: Place chicken on shredded lettuce or cooked somen noodles, if desired.

Oyako Donburi

yield: 4 servings

3 to 4 chicken thighs, skinless and boneless, sliced
1/3 onion, sliced
2 Tablespoons oil for frying
1/2 cup bamboo shoots, sliced and drained
1 can chicken broth (14-1/2-oz.)
4 Tablespoons shoyu
3 Tablespoons sugar
2 Tablespoons mirin
4 eggs, beaten

Heat oil and fry chicken and onions. Add chicken broth and bamboo shoots. Add shoyu, sugar and mirin. Add eggs, but do not stir. Cover and cook on medium-high heat until eggs are done.

Note: Expect a lot of liquid with 1 can of chicken broth. You may want to lessen the amount to 3/4 can broth to start with and add more. if desired.

· SEAFOOD ·

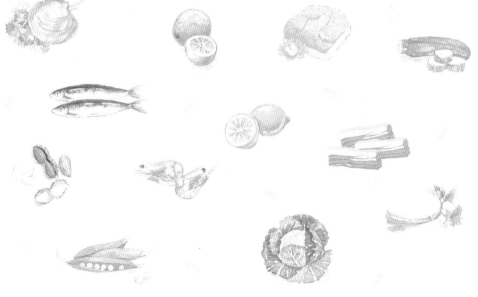

Seafood Tips

- Select fish with eyes that are bright, clear and bulging.
- Fish should be firm and elastic, springing back when touched.
- There should be no odor.
- Frozen fish should be tightly wrapped. If fish is discolored, it could indicate freezer burn.
- Avoid overcooking fish which makes it dry and tough. To test for doneness, place a fork in the thickest part of the fish. Gently twist the fork. Fish will flake easily when done.
- As a general guide, the cooking time of any fish, whole fish, steaks or fillets, is about 10 minutes for every inch of thickness. Measure the thickest part. The fish is done when it is opaque at the thickest part or slightly translucent at the center.
- The smaller the shrimp size, the higher the count per pound. The larger the shrimp, the higher the price.
  Jumbo   10 to 12 count
  Large   15 to 20
  Medium   26 to 30
  Small   40 to 50
- Allow about 1 pound of shrimp per serving. Shrimp is done when it turns pink and becomes firm. Cooking time will depend on the size of the shrimp.

Baked Fish

yield: 4 servings

2 pounds fish fillets
juice of 1 lemon
garlic salt and pepper to season
1 cup mayonnaise
1/4 cup finely chopped onion
bread crumbs for topping

Squeeze lemon juice on fish. Sprinkle with garlic salt and pepper. Place fish in a foil-lined baking pan. Mix mayonnaise and chopped onion together; spread on fish. Sprinkle with bread crumbs. Bake at 425°F for 20 to 25 minutes.

Note: Fish can be marinated overnight (without bread crumbs).

Salmon Teriyaki

yield: 4 servings

1 pound salmon steaks or fillets
1 Tablespoon oil

Marinade:
2 Tablespoons shoyu
1 Tablespoon mirin
1 teaspoon sugar
2 teaspoons sake

Cut salmon into serving portions and place in a bowl. Mix marinade ingredients in a small bowl; stir to dissolve sugar. Pour over salmon. Marinate for at least 15 minutes (save marinade.)

Fry salmon in heated oil in skillet and cook until light brown. Gently turn salmon over; cook for another 2 minutes, or until cooked through. Reduce heat to low; add marinade and cook for another minute.

Honey-Glazed Walnut Shrimp

yield: 4 servings

1/2 pound large shrimp or prawns
2 cups water
1 cup walnut halves
4 cups water
1/2 cup sugar
1/4 cup honey
oil for frying
2 egg whites, beaten
flour for coating
1/2 tablespoon vinegar
2 Tablespoons mayonnaise
1 Tablespoon sweetened condensed milk
1 Tablespoon sugar
1 Tablespoon roasted sesame seeds for garnish (optional)

Remove shells and veins from shrimp. Bring 2 cups water to boiling. Add walnuts; cook for 10 minutes. Drain.

Bring 4 cups water and 1/2 cup sugar to a boil. Add blanched walnuts and cook for 10 more minutes. Drain. Combine walnuts and honey. Heat oil in a wok and fry walnuts for 1 to 2 minutes or until brown.

Dip shrimp in egg whites; coat with flour. Heat oil in the wok and fry shrimp for 1 to 2 minutes. Remove shrimp and drain oil from wok. In the same hot wok, combine remaining ingredients; add shrimp and cook for 1 minute. Serve with walnuts.

Note: A local favorite that is gaining popularity in the fast food plate lunch venues.

Mimi's Shrimp

yield: 4 to 6 servings

3 pounds shrimp (21 to 25 count)

Marinade:
1 cup Canola oil
2 teaspoons shoyu
3 Tablespoons honey
3 teaspoons Hawaiian salt (pulverized with mortar and pestle)
2 cloves garlic, grated
dash of Tabasco™

Do not peel shrimp. Cut shrimp from back and remove vein. Butterfly shrimp and lay flat.

Mix together oil, shoyu, honey, pulverized Hawaiian salt and garlic. Add a few drops of Tabasco™. Keep stirring mixture as you dip each shrimp in the sauce. Lay flat in a pan for 1 hour. Grill on hibachi.

Note: Everyone always asks for this recipe after one taste! Our family knows this as Aunty Mimi's shrimp whenever they request it for family events and parties.

Tempura Mahimahi

yield: 2 to 4 servings

mahimahi fillet, cut into thin 2-inch slices
salt and pepper to season
1/2 cup Bisquick™
1/3 cup cold beer
panko flakes (fine)
oil for frying

Salt and pepper fish to taste. Mix Bisquick™ with beer. (Add more beer if batter is too thick.) Dip fish in batter, then roll in panko flakes. Fry in 1-inch hot oil until brown.

Miso Butterfish

yield: 4 servings

4 butterfish fillets
3/4 cup miso
1/3 cup sake or sherry

Paper towel dry butterfish. Mix miso and sake into a paste. Marinate fish in paste overnight. Broil until brown.

Note: Tastes wonderful and is so easy to prepare!

Opakapaka With Chinese Cabbage

yield: 2 to 4 servings

Opakapaka, whole fish, cleaned (size should fit in frying
  pan)
salt and pepper to season
flour for dredging
oil for frying fish
1 stalk green onion, finely chopped

Gravy with vegetable:
  2 Tablespoons chung choi, washed and chopped
  4 pieces shiitake mushrooms, soaked and sliced (save
    mushroom water)
  1 small head Chinese cabbage, cut in 1-1/4-inch slices
  1 piece each garlic and ginger, crushed
  1 teaspoon salt
  1 teaspoon shoyu
  1 teaspoon sugar
  1 cup mushroom water
  cornstarch mixed with equal amount water

Sprinkle salt and pepper on fish. Coat with flour and fry in hot oil. When fish is cooked, place on a serving platter and immediately sprinkle green onion over fish.

In the same frying pan used to cook fish, fry chung choi and mushrooms. Add Chinese cabbage. When almost done, add garlic, ginger, seasonings and mushroom water. Thicken with cornstarch and water mixture. Pour Chinese cabbage and gravy over fried fish.

Note: This is a very old recipe that my mom gave me and everyone loves it! The original recipe used mullet, but I prefer opakapaka. If I see fresh opakapaka at the supermarket the right size for my frying pan (Sometimes I'll cut off the tail to have it fit.) I'll change my menu for that night's meal and head for the produce department for Chinese cabbage.

Squid and Vegetables

yield: 4 servings

7 squids
1 package nishime kombu (1-oz.)
1 Tablespoon oil
1 clove garlic, crushed
1 stalk broccoli, cut into bite-size pieces
1 carrot, sliced thin, diagonally
1 stalk green onion, finely chopped

Sauce:
3 Tablespoons shoyu
2 Tablespoons rice vinegar
2 teaspoons cornstarch
2 Tablespoons water

Clean squid: Pull tentacles and draw out innards. Slit the body in half, lengthwise. Remove cartilage and rub off skin. Wash thoroughly.

Cut cleaned squid horizontally into 1-1/2-inch strips. Make slits on side which was cut.

Soak kombu in water for 5 minutes. Clean and cut into 1-inch pieces.

Heat pan. Add oil; brown garlic. Add squid, kombu and vegetables and stir-fry for about 3 minutes. Blend sauce ingredients; add to squid and vegetables. Cook together.

Mochiko Fish

yield: 4 to 6 servings

1 to 2 pounds mahimahi, or other white fish
2 Tablespoons oil

Marinade:
4 Tablespoons mochiko
4 Tablespoons cornstarch
2 Tablespoons flour
4 Tablespoons sugar
1 teaspoon salt
2 Tablespoons shoyu
1 egg, beaten
1 tablespoon chopped green onion
1 clove garlic, minced

Mix marinade ingredients. Marinate fish for 3 to 4 hours, or overnight, in refrigerator. Heat about 2 Tablespoons oil in a pan and fry fish on medium heat.

Chinese Steamed Fish

yield: 3 to 4 servings

3 pounds whole fish, cleaned with head and tail on
  shoyu to season
1/2 cup finely chopped green onion
1/4 cup finely chopped fresh ginger
1/4 cup finely chopped chung choi
1 cup peanut oil, heated

Pour small amount of shoyu in the cavity of the cleaned fish. Steam fish for 20 to 25 minutes in a steam pan. When fish is steamed, remove and place on a platter. Mix together green onion, ginger and chung choi and place over fish. Pour hot sizzling peanut oil over chopped ingredients and fish. Serve immediately.

Variation: If an elongated fish steamer pan is unavailable, chop fish into large pieces to fit in a bowl and place in a round-type steamer.

Note: Opakapaka (red snapper), kumu or other fish that steams well tastes best. A healthy and tasty alternative in preparing fish.

Shrimp Curry

yield: 3 to 5 servings

1-1/2 pounds shrimp, cleaned
1 onion, chopped
3 cloves garlic, minced
4 Tablespoons butter
2 cups water (or 1 can coconut milk and water to equal 2
    cups)
2 large tomatoes, peeled and chopped*
2 stalks celery, sliced
1 Tablespoon shredded coconut
1 piece ginger, crushed
1/4 teaspoon ground ginger
1 Tablespoon sugar
1-1/2 Tablespoons curry powder
1-1/2 Tablespoons flour
1-1/2 teaspoons salt
1/4 teaspoon pepper

Sauté onion and garlic in butter until lightly browned. Add water or coconut milk and bring to a boil. Add tomatoes, celery, coconut and fresh ginger. Blend ground ginger with sugar, curry powder, flour, salt and pepper. Add enough cold water to moisten into a paste and add to boiling mixture. Simmer, stirring occasionally, until vegetables are tender. Add shrimp; cook for 5 minutes.

Suggestion: Serve with condiments such as chutney, peanuts, boiled eggs, green onions or bacon bits.

Variation: Substitute shrimp with scallops or crab legs.

*To peel tomatoes, place tomatoes in boiling water for 1 to 2 minutes. Remove and cool in cold water. Skin can then be easily peeled off.

Shrimp Scampi

yield: 4 to 6 servings

2 pounds large shrimp (16 to 20 count)
2 Tablespoons olive oil
1/4 cup butter
3 cloves garlic, minced
1 Tablespoon lemon juice
1 teaspoon salt
dash of pepper
2 stalks green onion, thinly sliced
2 Tablespoons minced parsley
lemon wedges for garnish, optional

Shell and clean shrimp, leaving tail on. Combine olive oil and butter in a frying pan; heat until butter melts. Add garlic, lemon juice, salt, pepper and green onion. Heat over medium-high heat. Add shrimp and stir until shrimp is cooked, about 2 minutes. Do Not Overcook. Remove to serving platter. Sprinkle with parsley and garnish with lemon wedges, if desired.

Broccoli With Shrimp

yield: 4 servings

1/2 pound jumbo shrimp (16 to 20 count)
broccoli (slender stalks with flower head, 3-1/2-inch
  lengths)
1 teaspoon baking soda
2 Tablespoons cornstarch
1/2 cup water
2 Tablespoons oil
1 teaspoon salt
pinch of curry powder
oil for deep frying (about 2-inches deep)

Gravy:
  1/2 cup water
  2 teaspoons sugar
  dash of sesame seed oil
  1 Tablespoon cornstarch mixed with 1 Tablespoon water

Peel shrimp and remove vein. Slit a little opening through middle of shrimp, just wide enough for broccoli to pass through. Mix baking soda, 2 Tablespoons cornstarch and 1/2 cup water; mix thoroughly with shrimp. Add 2 Tablespoons oil, salt and curry powder; mix thoroughly. Marinate for 15 minutes.

Slice broccoli tips slant-cut. (Cut lengthwise in half if broccoli is thick.) Push broccoli through the slit in the shrimp. Heat oil on medium to medium-high heat and deep-fry a batch of shrimp and broccoli for 30 seconds. Remove and put in a container. Add another batch to cook. Repeat until all shrimp and broccoli are cooked.

In a frying pan, heat gravy (except cornstarch mixture). Stir in cornstarch mixture until gravy thickens. Mix in cooked shrimp and broccoli, toss together and serve hot.

Note: This dish was a favorite of ours at the Yong Sing Restaurant (now just a memory) where the Au clan held our traditional annual Christmas party.

Shrimp With Black Bean Sauce

yield: 4 servings

1 pound shrimp, peeled
1 Tablespoon oil
1 onion, cut into 1-inch pieces
1 green pepper, seeded and cubed
salt to season
2 cloves garlic, crushed
green onion, chopped, or Chinese parsley for garnish
   (optional)

Sauce:
1 clove garlic, minced
1 teaspoon grated fresh ginger
2 Tablespoons rinsed and mashed salted black beans
1 Tablespoon sherry
1 Tablespoon shoyu
1/2 cup chicken broth
1 teaspoon sugar
2 teaspoons cornstarch with 1 Tablespoon water
dash of sesame seed oil

In a frying pan or wok, heat oil and stir-fry onion and bell pepper with a sprinkle of salt, until vegetables are crisp-tender. Remove. In the same pan, add a little oil as needed and sauté garlic. Add shrimp; cook until pink. Remove shrimp and discard garlic.

In the same pan, add a little oil as needed, and sauté minced garlic, ginger and black bean. Add sherry, shoyu, chicken broth and sugar. Bring to a boil; stir in cornstarch mixture and sesame seed oil. When sauce thickens, add reserved onion, pepper and shrimp. Heat through and serve. Garnish with green onion or Chinese parsley.

Fish With Somen

yield: 2 to 4 servings

1-1/2 pounds whole fish (ehu, onaga, kumu), scaled and
cleaned
1 package somen (9-oz.), cooked according to instructions
on package
1 stalk green onion, finely chopped

Sauce:
    1/2 cup shoyu
    1/3 cup water
    3 Tablespoons sugar
    2 Tablespoons sake
    1-inch piece ginger, crushed

Combine sauce ingredients in a saucepan large enough to hold fish; bring to a
boil. Place fish in sauce, cover and cook on medium-low heat for 10 to 12 minutes, or until done. Baste fish occasionally with shoyu sauce. Carefully place
fish on a serving platter.

Twirl somen into individual serving portions and arrange around fish. Sprinkle
with green onion. Strain shoyu sauce and serve in a separate bowl.

*Note: My mom uses 2 to 3 ti leaves under the fish as it cooks. Then, by hold-
ing both ends of the ti leaves, she easily lifts the cooked fish out and onto the
serving platter. (This dish has been a tradition at our New Year's party ever
since I was a little girl and my mom still cooks this every year.)*

Lobster With Black Bean Sauce

yield: 2 servings

1 lobster tail (about 3/4 to 1 pound)
1 Tablespoon oil
salt to season
1 slice fresh ginger, crushed
1 clove garlic, crushed
3/4 cup chicken broth
2 teaspoons cornstarch mixed with 1 Tablespoon water
2 Tablespoons finely chopped green onions
Chinese parsley for garnish (optional)

Seasoning:
3 Tablespoons rinsed and mashed salted black beans
1 Tablespoon liquor
1/4 teaspoon sesame oil
1 Tablespoon oyster sauce
1/2 teaspoon hoisin sauce
1/2 teaspoon salt

Mix seasoning ingredients in a bowl and set aside.

Chop unshelled lobster into sections. Heat oil in pan. Add salt, ginger and garlic. Put lobster tail in and fry for a minute. Add seasoning and sauté for a minute more. Add chicken broth and cover. Cook for 3 minutes; then stir and cook another 3 minutes. Thicken with cornstarch mixture. Add green onions. Garnish with Chinese parsley, if desired.

Curried Lobster With Fried Haupia

yield: 4 servings

8-ounce lobster tail, remove shell and cut into 1-1/2-inch cubes
1/3 cup carrots, cut into small pieces
3 Tablespoons frozen peas
1/2 potato, cut into 1-inch cubes and soaked in water
2 Tablespoons oil
3 Tablespoons diced onion
1/2 cup chicken broth
1/4 cup coconut milk
2 Tablespoons half-and-half cream
2 to 3 Tablespoons curry powder
1/8 teaspoon salt
1/8 teaspoon pepper
2 to 3 Tablespoons raisins
2 Tablespoons cornstarch mixed with 2 Tablespoons chicken broth
8 deep-fried haupia pieces (see recipe on next page)

Boil carrots until just done. Add peas just to blanch. Drain. Set aside.

Drain potato and pat dry with paper towel. Deep fry potato for 2 minutes on medium heat or until cooked. Set aside.

In a small bowl, combine chicken broth, coconut milk, half-and-half cream, curry powder, salt and pepper: mix together. Set aside.

Heat a wok or pan on high heat, add oil, then reduce heat slightly. Stir-fry onion and lobster for 2 minutes or until cooked thoroughly. Add chicken broth mixture. Stir-fry for 1 minute more. Stir cornstarch mixture into the wok. Add potatoes, carrots, peas and raisins. Bring to a boil. (Add more chicken broth, if desired, so gravy is of desired consistency.)

Transfer to a serving dish and garnish with deep-fried haupia on the side.

(See recipe on next page)

Fried Haupia

yield: ? servings

1-1/2 cups coconut milk
3/4 cup water
1/3 cup sugar
5 Tablespoons cornstarch

Egg Wash:
1 egg
1 cup water
1 tablespoon flour

3 Tablespoons cornstarch for dusting
oil for deep-frying

In a double boiler, heat coconut milk. Stir together water, sugar and 5 Tablespoons cornstarch until smooth. Stir into coconut milk and cook over low heat until thickened, stirring constantly. Increase temperature slightly and stir vigorously to prevent burning. Mixture should be thick. Pour mixture into an 8-inch square pan. Refrigerate to set.

Cut haupia into 24 pieces, each 2x1-1/2-inches. Dip in egg wash, dust with cornstarch and deep fry for 2 minutes. Place haupia around curried lobster. (Since only 8 fried haupia is needed, you can choose to fry the rest or keep the remainder as is.)

Note: We first tasted this fabulous dish at my brother-in-law's wedding reception 14 years ago and we have enjoyed it ever since. My nephew had this at his reception last year and has tried this recipe several times, sometimes using shrimp for the lobster. The fried haupia is a perfect complement to the spicy lobster curry.

Mahimahi Bake

yield: 8 to 10 servings

1 pound mahimahi, cut into small bite-size pieces
1 tray bay shrimp (about 8-oz.)
1 tray or package imitation crab meat (10-oz.)
1/2 onion, chopped
1 stalk celery, chopped
3 stalks green onion, chopped
salt and pepper to season
mayonnaise to moisten (about 2 heaping Tablespoons)
1/4 cup melted margarine
paprika for sprinkling

Combine first six ingredients. Sprinkle with salt and pepper. Add enough mayonnaise to keep moist. Place mixture in a greased baking pan. Drizzle with margarine and sprinkle with paprika. Bake at 350°F for 20 minutes. Let stand for 5 to 10 minutes before serving.

Variation: Substitute 3 or 4 lobster tails for fish. Shell and chop lobster into bite-size pieces.

Suggestion: The next day, place chilled Mahimahi Bake on a bed of lettuce and tomatoes for a great-tasting salad.

Lomi Salmon

yield: 8 to 10 servings

1 pound salted salmon
5 large ripe tomatoes, diced
1 medium onion, finely chopped
3 to 4 stalks green onion, finely sliced

Soak salmon in cold water for 1 hour, longer if very salty. Remove skin and bones and shred or cut into small pieces. Combine all ingredients and "lomi" (massage with fingers). Chill for 2 hours.

 Quick and Easy

Wiki-Wiki Creamed Tuna

yield: 2 servings

1 can cream of mushroom soup (10-3/4 oz.)
1/2 can or water (use mushroom soup can)
1 can tuna (6-oz.), drained
1/2 cup frozen or canned peas, carrots or corn
salt and pepper to season (optional)

Place contents of mushroom soup with 1/2 can of water. Add tuna. Simmer on low heat. Add vegetables just before serving. Season with salt and pepper, if desired. Best served on hot rice.

Butterfish With Shoyu Sauce

yield: 3 to 4 servings

1 pound butterfish
salt and pepper to season
flour for dredging

Sauce:
1/4 cup shoyu
5 Tablespoons sugar
1 stalk green onion, chopped
1 large clove garlic, minced
chili pepper or crushed red pepper to season (optional)

Combine sauce ingredients and mix well.

Salt and pepper butterfish. Dredge in flour and fry. When done, soak in sauce while still hot. Serve or simmer in sauce for a few minutes before serving.

Note: My mom gave me this recipe and I really like it!

Squid Luau

yield: 6 to 8 servings

2 pounds taro (luau) leaves
1-1/2 pounds squid or tako, cut into bite-size pieces
2 teaspoons salt
water
1 can coconut milk

Clean taro leaves and discard stems. Cook in boiling water for 2 hours, or until it reaches desired consistency; drain. Clean squid and slice in rings. Simmer squid in 1 cup water and 1 teaspoon salt until tender; drain. Mix squid and cooked luau leaves together. Add coconut milk and cook over low heat until done. Add more salt to taste, if necessary.

Note: Clean squid by pulling tentacles and drawing out innards of the squid.. Remove cartilage and rub off skin. Wash thoroughly. Slice in 1/4-inch rings.

Furikake Salmon

yield: 2 servings

1 fillet of salmon
mayonnaise for spreading
furikake for sprinkling
1 tablespoon butter

Cut fillet into portion sizes. Generously spread mayonnaise on one side of salmon. Sprinkle furikake generously over mayonnaise. Heat pan on medium heat and add butter. Place salmon, furikake side down, lower heat to medium-low and slowly cook for 10 to 15 minutes. Turn over and repeat previous steps.

Optional: If desired, serve cooked salmon with the following sauce.

Sauce:
2 Tablespoons butter
2 cloves garlic, minced
1/4 cup shoyu
2 Tablespoons sugar

Melt butter, add garlic and stir. Blend in shoyu and sugar and simmer for 1 to 2 minutes. Pour over cooked salmon.

Note: This is a local-style salmon that is so tasty. Thanks to Donna Watanabe who gave me this recipe.

Black Bean Salmon Head

yield: 2 servings

2 pounds fresh salmon head, rinsed and cut into 2-inch
pieces

Sauce:
2 Tablespoons salted black beans
3 cloves garlic
2 Tablespoons cornstarch
2 Tablespoons shoyu
1 Tablespoon sugar
2 Tablespoons oyster sauce
2 Tablespoons sesame oil
1 Tablespoon sherry

Rinse black beans 2 to 3 times. Mince black beans and garlic together to form a paste. Combine paste with remaining ingredients. Marinate fish head with sauce for a minimum of 3 hours. Steam for 20 to 30 minutes until cooked. Do not overcook.

Variation: Substitute salmon with sea bass fish head.

Note: Ask the seafood person at the supermarket to cut the salmon head into pieces as it is quite hard to do.

Local Style Fish Casserole

yield: 8 to 10 servings

3 pounds fillet of fish (mahimahi, aku, or swordfish)
3/4 cup white wine
2 cloves garlic, minced
1 onion, thinly sliced
1/4 cup butter
1 Portuguese sausage (10-oz.), sliced
1 eggplant (long type), sliced
salt and pepper to season
1 tray fresh mushrooms (8-oz.),sliced
1/2 cup mayonnaise
breadcrumbs to sprinkle

Cut fish fillet into bite-size pieces; soak in wine and garlic for 30 minutes. In foil-lined 9x13-inch pan, place onion slices and dab butter here and there on onion. Next, layer in order: Portuguese sausage, eggplant and fish. Sprinkle salt and pepper on fish. Cover fish with mayonnaise. Layer mushrooms over. Sprinkle breadcrumbs on top and bake at 425°F for 20 minutes.

Note: On one of my visits to Hilo to research recipes there, two of my Hilo High friends, Aileen Kaneshiro and Lilian Takemura, gave me this recipe which they say their Hilo friends and relatives really enjoy.

· OTHERS ·

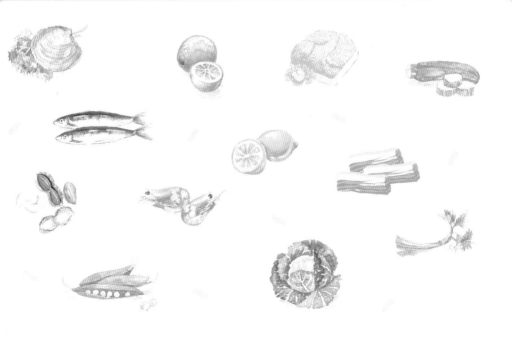

Jook (Chinese Rice Porridge)

yield: 8 to 10 servings

3 cups uncooked rice
2 Tablespoons Hawaiian salt
2 Tablespoons oil
1 cup (skinned) raw peanuts

Soup Mixture:
1-1/2 quarts water
3 ham hocks
1 turkey carcass and bones
2 cubes chicken bouillon

Garnish:
1/2 cup finely minced chung choi
2 stalks green onion, finely cut
Chinese parsley, finely cut
shredded lettuce
shredded turkey or ham

Rinse rice; drain. Marinate in salt and oil; set aside.

In a large pot, combine soup mixture ingredients; boil for 1 hour. Remove bones and strain liquid to remove small pieces of residue. Place strained broth back into the pot. Add water until it measures 1-1/2 quarts of combined liquid. Add marinated rice and raw peanuts. Bring to a boil and simmer on medium-low heat for 2 hours, stirring every 15 to 30 minutes. Serve with garnishes. Place each garnish in separate bowls for individual selection.

Chow Fun Noodles

yield: 10 to 12 servings

4 sheets look fun noodles
oil for stir-frying
Hawaiian salt to taste
1 medium carrot, julienne cut
1 small onion, cut in half, thinly sliced
2 stalks celery, julienne cut
1/2 pound Chinese peas
1 package bean sprout mixture (12-oz.)
1 pound char siu, julienne cut

Sauce:
3 Tablespoons shoyu
3 Tablespoons oyster sauce
1/2 teaspoon sugar

Cut look fun into 1/2-inch strips. In a wok, heat oil and Hawaiian salt. Lightly stir-fry carrots, onion, celery, peas and bean sprouts, each separately. (Add more oil and salt as needed.) Set aside. Stir-fry char siu and set aside. Mix look fun sauce with look fun noodles. Add remaining ingredients and toss.

Jai (Monk's Food)

yield: 10 to 12 servings

Mixture A:

3 packages foo jook (dried bean curd) (7-oz. each), soak until softened, cut into 3-inch lengths

3 cups soaked and cleaned black fungus

2 cups hairy seaweed (fat choi), soak until softened, drain

1 cup lily flower, soaked until plump, drain and pinch off hard tip

2 cups dried mushroom, soak, cut into 1-1/2-inch x 1-1/2 inch pieces

Hawaiian salt for stir-fry

oil for stir-fry

water or chicken broth

Mixture B:

1 jar red bean sauce(16-oz.), mash with 1/2 cup brown sugar

1/2 cup soaked, drained lotus seed (lin chee)

1/2 pound fresh water chestnut (ma tai), peeled, cut into 1/4-inch slices

3 packages fried tofu, cut into 1x 2-inch pieces

1 cup oyster sauce (more or less to your preference)

4 pieces fresh ginger, slivered

Mixture C:

2 pounds won bok, cut into 1-inch wide strips

3 cans chai pow yu (fried gluten) (10-oz. each)

2 cans bamboo shoots (10-oz. each)

4 packages long rice (2-oz. each)

2 cans gingko nuts (10-oz. each)

Garnish:

roasted sesame seeds

Chinese parsley

Stir-fry mixture A ingredients in oil and Hawaiian salt. Place all ingredients in a large pot and add water to cover. Boil for 1/2 hour. Add Mixture B ingredients. Boil for another 1/2 hour. Add water if needed to cover ingredients. Add Mixture C ingredients and boil another 1/2 hour. Serve with garnishes.

Note: If using chicken broth in place of water, decrease amount of Hawaiian salt when stir-frying. A Chinese vegetarian recipe that was shared by Audrey Au and passed down for three generations. This dish is usually made in large quantities during the Chinese New Year's celebration and given to family and friends. It requires a lot of preparation but tastes so good that the effort is well worth it. Hint: It can be frozen in serving-sized portion for at least 6 months.

Corned Beef Hash Patties

yield: 4 to 6 servings

1 can corned beef
3 to 4 medium potatoes
1/4 cup minced onions
3 eggs, beaten
salt and pepper to season
Chinese parsley, minced (optional)
Flour for dredging
Oil for frying

Cut potatoes in half; boil in enough water until soft. Peel skin and mash in bowl. Add corned beef, onions, eggs and seasoning. Mix together. Form into patties; dredge in flour. Heat pan on medium heat; add about 1-2 Tablespoons oil. Fry patties, adding oil as needed.

Note: This is my Aunty Fusako Martinez's recipe and whenever she makes this for potluck nothing is left!

Linguine With White Clam Sauce

yield: 5 to 6 servings

1/2 cup butter

1/4 cup olive oil

6 to 8 cloves garlic, minced or pressed

3 cans chopped clams (6-1/2 oz. each)

1 cup parsley flakes

1 teaspoon oregano

1 teaspoon basil

1/4 teaspoon crushed red pepper

1 package linguine (16-oz.), cooked according to package instructions

Melt butter in olive oil. Add garlic; cook until golden. (Do not burn garlic!) Add clams with liquid and rest of ingredients. Simmer for 5 minutes. Toss mixture with cooked linguine.

Gon Lo Mein

yield: 10 to 12 servings

2 pounds fried chow mein noodles
1/4 cup oyster sauce
1/4 cup sesame oil
oil for stir-frying
Hawaiian salt to season
1/4 pound char siu, slivered for garnish
Chinese parsley, for garnish

Vegetables:
1 small onion, slivered
2 stalks celery, julienne cut
1 small carrot, julienne cut
1/4 pound snow peas
1 package bean sprout mixture (12-oz.)
6 dried black mushrooms, softened in water, sliced

Combine chow mein noodles with oyster sauce and sesame oil and marinate for 1 hour. In a heavy frying pan or wok, heat oil and stir-fry noodles. Set aside.

Stir-fry lightly each vegetable separately in oil and Hawaiian salt (except mushroom). Set aside. Stir-fry mushroom without salt and add back all ingredients (except char siu and Chinese parsley) into the pan and toss together. Place on platter and garnish with char siu and Chinese parsley.

Note: Always a local favorite in any potluck gathering.

Baked Gon Lo Mein

yield: 4 to 6 servings

1 package chow mein noodles (12-oz.)
1/2 package bean sprouts (half of 10-oz.)
1 cup celery, sliced thin diagonally
1/2 cup green onion, cut in 1/2-inch lengths
1 cup slivered char siu
1 Tablespoon roasted sesame seeds
2 Tablespoons oyster sauce
1 Tablespoon sesame oil
Chinese parsley, chopped, for garnish

Mix noodles with vegetables, char siu and sesame seeds in a 9x13-inch pan. Toss with oyster sauce and sesame oil. Cover with foil. Bake at 350°F for 15 to 20 minutes. Garnish with Chinese parsley before serving.

Note: Try it. It's quite good for a quick and easy way to prepare Gon Lo Mein.

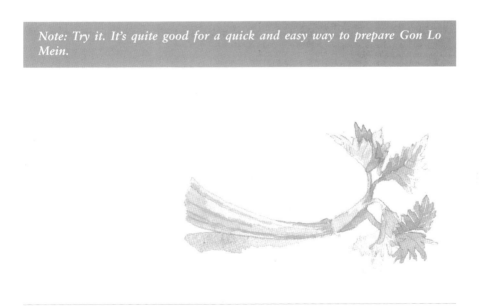

Long Rice and Vegetables

yield: 4 servings

2 packages long rice (1-3/4-oz. each)
1/2 can chicken broth (half of 14-1/2-oz)
1 cup water
1 Tablespoon oil and 1/2 teaspoon sesame oil
1 clove garlic, chopped
1/2-inch slice fresh ginger
2 shiitake mushrooms, soaked and sliced
1 carrot, slivered
1/4 onion, sliced
2 stalks green onion, cut in 2-inch lengths
1/2 teaspoon salt

Sauce:
1/2 can chicken broth
1 Tablespoon mirin
1 Tablespoon shoyu
1 teaspoon oyster sauce
1/2 teaspoon sugar

Boil long rice in 1/2 can chicken broth and 1 cup water for 3 minutes. Drain and set aside. Cut into 3-inch lengths.

Stir-fry garlic and ginger in oil. Add vegetables and salt. Cook until tender. Mix sauce ingredients and add to vegetables. Remove ginger. Add Long rice. Cook for 2 minutes.

Variation: Add cooked shredded chicken (i.e., left-over shoyu chicken is good) to long rice.

Nishime

yield: 6 to 8 servings

4 pieces chicken thighs, boneless and skinless
1 Tablespoon oil
1 can chicken broth (14-1/2-oz.)
4 pieces dried mushrooms, soaked and sliced
1 package nishime konbu (1-oz.)
1 container konyaku (10-oz.), cut in 3/4x1-inch pieces
1 can bamboo shoots, (8-1/2-oz.), cut in 1-inch pieces
1/4 cup shoyu
1/3 cup sugar (or less)
2 to 3 carrots, cut in 1-inch pieces
1 small turnip, (about 1/2 pound), cut in 1-inch pieces
1 cup burdock root (gobo)
2 cups araimo, peeled and cut into 1-1/2-inch pieces
1 can lotus root (7-oz.), or 1/2 pound fresh lotus root,
   optional
1 package aburage (2-oz.), cut in 1-1/2-inch pieces
1/4 pound chinese peas, blanched

Soak mushrooms in water until soft; slice. Wash konbu and tie into knots leaving 1-inch apart. Cut between knots. Scrape burdock root clean and cut into 1/4-inch thick diagonal slices and soak in water until ready to use.

Cut chicken into bite-sized pieces. In large pot, fry chicken in oil until light brown. Add chicken broth, mushrooms, konbu, konyaku and bamboo shoots. Cover and cook for 10 minutes. Add shoyu and sugar, cover, and cook for 5 minutes. Add carrots, turnips and gobo, cover, and cook for 15 minutes. Add araimo and lotus root, if desired. Cover, and cook until taro is fork-tender. Toss in aburage and Chinese peas. Mix together and serve.

Macaroni (Ziti) and Cheese

yield: 6 to 8 servings

1 package ziti or elbow macaroni (16-oz.)
1 package cubed cheddar cheese (24-oz.)

Sauce:
1 can evaporated milk, (12-oz.)
1 cup water
2 cups sour cream
1 container cottage cheese (8-oz.)
1/2 cup butter, melted
1/2 cup flour

Cook ziti according to package directions. Mix sauce ingredients, blending butter and flour last. In a large roasting pan, layer ziti on bottom, cubed cheese next and then sauce on top. Bake at 350°F, uncovered, for 1 hour.

Note: For cheese lovers! This is a hearty and rich baked macaroni and cheese. My neighbor, Molly, really liked this and told her sister about it.

Note: Thank you to Mardee Domingo Melton, who got this recipe from her sister-in-law, and who then shared it with me.

Portuguese Bean Soup

yield: 8 to 10 servings

1-2 pounds smoked ham hock or ham shank
3 cans chicken broth
2 cans kidney beans (15-oz. each)
2 cans tomato sauce (8-oz. each)
1 clove garlic, crushed
1 teaspoon pepper
1 medium onion, chopped
4 potatoes, cubed into 1-1/2-inch pieces
4 carrots, cut into 1-1/2-inch pieces
1 Portuguese sausage (10-oz.), cut in 1/2-inch slices
1 bay leaf
1 small head cabbage

In a large pot, cover ham hock with chicken broth. Add enough water to cover and boil until tender (about 1 to 2 hours.) Skim off fat while cooking. Add rest of ingredients and cook until tender. Continue to skim off fat.

Note: Great to cook ahead and serve the next day. My neighbor, Darleen Dyer, who serves this often for "potluck," says she triples this recipe so she can save some for her husband.

Tripe Stew

yield: 6 servings

2 pounds honeycomb tripe
3 Tablespoons baking soda
4 medium carrots, cut into 1/2-inch pieces
3 potatoes, cut in 1-inch pieces
1 large onion, cut into chunks
1 bell pepper, cut into 1-inch pieces
1 stem celery, cut into 1-inch pieces
3 cans tomato sauce (8-oz. each)
4 cups water
4 to 5 Tablespoons cornstarch mixed with equal amount of
   water, for thickening
Hawaiian salt to season

Rinse tripe. Sprinkle baking soda on tripe and rub all over. Rinse and place tripe in a pot. Cover with water and parboil for 30 minutes. Drain and cool. Cut tripe into small strips (1/2x2-inches).

Bring tomato sauce and 4 cups water to a boil. Add tripe and vegetables and cook for 30 minutes or until vegetables are done. Thicken with cornstarch mixture. Add salt to taste.

Note: A local favorite! Requires a little preparation but is well worth the effort.

Spanish Rice

yield: 6 to 8 servings

1 pound lean ground beef
1 to 2 cloves garlic, minced
1 small onion, chopped
1 Tablespoon oil
1 green pepper, chopped
2 Tablespoons chili powder
1/2 teaspoon salt
1/4 teaspoon pepper
1/2 teaspoon oregano
1 can stewed tomatoes (14-1/2-oz.)
1 can pitted olives (6-oz.), undrained, keep whole or cut in
   slices
1-1/2 cups uncooked rice, rinsed and drained

In a large skillet, heat oil and sauté garlic and onions. Add ground beef, green pepper, chili powder, salt, pepper and oregano. Cook until ground beef is done. Add rice and cook for 3 minutes. Add stewed tomatoes, breaking up tomatoes into smaller pieces. Mix in olives with liquid. Add just enough water to cover. Simmer with lid on until rice is cooked, taking care not to burn rice (about 40 minutes or until done.) Stir occasionally while cooking.

Note: Thanks to Gaylynn Kalama for sharing this ono "Spanish Rice" with all of us at Aikahi Elementary.

Tofu Burgers

yield: 4 to 6 servings

1 block firm tofu (20-oz)
1/2 cup finely grated carrot
1/4 cup finely chopped onion
1 slice bread, crumbled
1 egg
1 Tablespoon chopped green onion (chives or parsley)
oil for frying

Use cheesecloth or clean cotton towel to squeeze tofu dry. Mix with other ingredients. Make patties. Heat a little oil in a pan and cook like burgers.

Note: Top with a slice of cheese or brush on teriyaki-type sauce.

Steamed Egg Custard

yield: 4 servings

4 eggs, beaten

5 dried scallops (approximately 1-inch in diameter), soaked, shredded (optional)

1 Tablespoon shoyu

2 Tablespoons oil

1 teaspoon salt

1 cup hot water (not boiling)

Mix all ingredients (except hot water). Carefully mix in hot water and pour mixture into a bowl for steaming. Skim off bubbles on top of mixture. Steam for 20 minutes on medium heat, or until custard is cooked. Do not overcook. Bubbles will form when overcooked.

Note: A family style side dish that is considered "comfort food" on the Chinese menu.

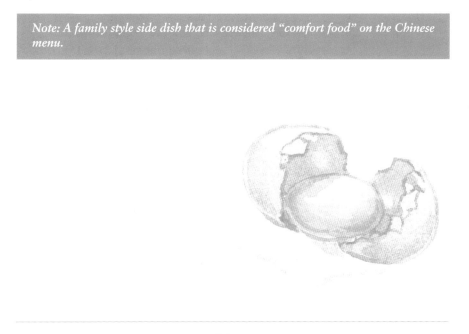

Won Ton Soup

yield: 5 to 6 servings

1 pound won ton wrappers
2 cans chicken broth (14-1/2-oz. each)
1/2 pound char siu, slivered for garnish
Chinese parsley for garnish
3 quarts water

Filling:
1 pound ground pork
1/2 pound shrimp, cleaned and chopped
1/2 cup finely minced water chestnut
1 teaspoon Hawaiian salt
1 teaspoon sesame oil
1 teaspoon shoyu
1/2 teaspoon oyster sauce
1/2 teaspoon sugar
1/2 teaspoon cornstarch

Combine filling ingredients and mix well. Place 1 teaspoon of pork filling on won ton wrapper. Wet edges and fold into a triangle. Wet left side of won ton skin. Pull sides back and pinch together, placing one side on top of the sealer.

Boil 3 quarts water rapidly. Place 10 won tons into boiling water. Won tons are cooked when they float to the top. Repeat procedure until all are cooked. Rinse in cold water as they are removed

Place in soup bowls and pour heated chicken broth over won ton. Garnish with char siu and Chinese parsley.

Glossary

aburage	deep-fried tofu, fried bean curd
adobo	vinegar-flavored meat
aku	skipjack tuna, bonito or katsuo
araimo	dasheen, Japanese taro
bitter melon	balsam melon
black beans	dau see, salted and fermented black beans
char siu	red roast pork, roasted sweet red pork
Chinese parsley	cilantro
choi sum	Chinese broccoli
chow mein	fried noodles
chung choi	chung choi, preserved salted turnip
daikon	white radish or turnip
dashi-no-moto	powdered oriental seasoning
five spices powder	blend of Chinese star anise, cloves, fennel, peppercorns and cinnamon
dau see	salted and fermented black beans
furikake	rice condiment
gobo	burdock root
haupia	coconut cornstarch pudding
Hawaiian salt	coarse sea salt
hoisin	spicy bean sauce
kamaboko	steamed fishcake
kalbi	Korean barbecued short ribs, khal bi
ko choo jung	Korean sauce made from mochi rice and chili peppers
konyaku	tuber root flour cake
kumu	goatfish
laulau	steamed bundle of meat in ti leaves

lomi	massage, rub or crush ingredients with fingers
lomi salmon	salted salmon and tomatoes
long rice	translucent mung bean noodles
look fun	wide sheets of Chinese noodles
luau leaves	taro leaves
lup cheong	Chinese sweet pork sausage
mahimahi	dolphinfish
mirin	sweet rice wine
miso	fermented soybean paste
mochiko	glutinous rice flour
nishime	cooked vegetable dish
nishime konbu	narrow kelp used in nishime
opakapaka	pink snapper
oyster sauce	oyster-flavored sauce
panko	flour meal for breading
sake	rice wine
shiitake	dried mushrooms
shoyu	soy sauce
sin choi	pickled mustard cabbage
sukiyaki	vegetable and meat dish
tako	octopus
teriyaki	soy-flavored sauce
tempura	fritters
ti leaf	broad leaf of ti plant
tofu	fresh soybean curd
tortilla	Mexican flat bread made of cornmeal or wheat flour
wok	Chinese fry pan
wonbok	Chinese cabbage, makina, napa
yakitori	Japanese-style grilled chicken

Index

Mochiko Fish, 112
Opakapaka With Chinese Cabbage, 110
Salmon Teriyaki, 106
Tempura Mahimahi, 109
Wiki Wiki Creamed Tuna, 123
Five Spices Shoyu Chicken, 76
Flavored Chicken for Chinese Stir-Fry, 82
Fried Chicken, 84
Furikake Salmon, 126

G
Gon Lo Mein, 136
Goulash, 24
Green Beans
Lu-Bee, 38
Pork Sari Sari, 51
Green Pepper
Beef Tomato, 6
Chicken Cacciatore, 74
Chopped Steak, 5
Shish Kabob, 13
Shrimp With Black Bean Sauce, 117
Ground Beef
Baked Spaghetti, 18
Barbecued Meat Balls, 27
Crescent Roll Tacos, 21
Goulash, 24
Hamburger Steak With Gravy, "Loco Moco" Style, 10
Easy Beef Stroganoff,
Hawaiian Teriyaki Burger, 26
Lasagne, 31
Meatloaf, 24
Stuffed Cabbage Rolls, 29
Tofu With Ground Beef and Miso, 17
Wiki Wiki Chili, 15

Ground Pork
Aburage Stuffed With Pork Hash, 52
Pork Hash, 63
Spicy Eggplant With Pork, 61
Pork Hash, 63
Stuffed Bitter Melon, 56
Won Ton Soup, 146

H
Hamburger Steak With Gravy "Loco Moco" Style, 10
Easy Beef Stroganoff, 26
Harm Ha Pork, 64
Hawaiian Teriyaki Burger, 32
Herb-Crusted Rack of Lamb, 37
Honey-Glazed Walnut Shrimp, 107

I
Italian Chicken, 86

J
Jai, (Monk's Food), 132
Jook, (Chinese Rice Porridge), 130
Jumbo's Restaurant's Beef Stew, 9

K
Kalbi, 19
Kau Yuk, 48

L
Lamb Main Dishes
Herb-Crusted Rack of Lamb, 37
Lamb Shish Kabob, 41
Lamb Stew With Peanuts, 40
Lu-Bee (Green Beans With Lamb), 38
McCarthy's Marinade, 39
Roast Lamb, 42